Stoicism for Business

Ancient stoic wisdom and practical advice for building mental toughness, productivity habits and success in modern management!

R. Stevens

book.

By reading this document, the reader agrees that under no circumstances is the author responsible for any losses, direct or indirect, which are incurred as a result of the use of the information contained within this document, including, but not limited to, — errors, omissions, or inaccuracies.

Hello fellow stoic,

We live in a stressful and fast-paced business world.

When reading information for the first time, everything seems logical and clear, but when surrounded by distractions at work, we tend to forget quickly and move on as usual.

We forget things because we have to process a lot of new information every single day and we don´t actively repeat the lessons we have learned.

We have found not 1 but 2 practical and 'stoic' solutions for you.

Quotes

The book is full of quotes from the ancient Stoics and from modern-day business people. A quote is an ideal medium, to deliver an important story or message in a very compact way. Only messages that get repeated will make it to our long-term memory.

3-Month-Self-Evaluation-Journal

It will take time, Self-Awareness and Self-Evaluation to change yourself. A journal is one of the best ways to evaluate and improve yourself and a constant basis. Journaling is used by a lot of successful people to continuously grow and learn.

So my advice is to print the quotes and the ´3-Month-Self-Evaluation Journal´ used in ´Stoicism for Business´. Tape these quotes on your computer screen or on the bathroom mirror. A great way for a daily reminder for your personal road to more success and to hit the next level in your business. Print the Self-Evaluation Journal to help yourself transform in the coming 3 months.

If you want to be productive:

- Go to: https://businessleadershipplatform.com/stoic-quotes-business-pdf

- Get the 3-Month-Stoic-Self-Evaluation-Journal and the quotes
- print both
- start reading

Enjoy the book.

R. Stevens

Table of Contents

Introduction

The Basics of Stoicism

"Stoicism is the wisdom of madness and cynicism, the madness of wisdom." -Bergen Evans

The word 'Stoic' is often misused in today's world, whereas the term would once refer to an almost sacred form of Greek philosophy, the modern-day usage has turned Stoicism into a building block of the composition of an emotionless shell, the opposite of empathy and compassion, a fact which often causes the term to be misconstrued as a negative state of being, much like cynicism.

In other words, this use of the term 'Stoic' is much like the modern-day use of the word 'sick' – what it actually means, and what it is used to refer to are two very different things.

So, what is actual 'Stoicism'?

Why don't we dip into its history a bit, before we answer that question?

Stoicism: A History

The entire concept of Stoicism actually stemmed from the ancient Greek concept of *cynicism*, which ironically, is yet another philosophical doctrine that is greatly misconstrued in modern usage. Historically, *cynicism* was an 'ethical doctrine' which deemed the attainment and adaptation of complete virtue to be the true purpose of life. The idea being that all conventional desires that a person may have in regard to their 'worldly' persona; be it health, wealth, power or fame were all to be rejected as much as possible but for the bare necessities required to sustain natural life. So as to minimize worldly suffering and move towards the ultimate goal of happiness.

Zeno of Citium was a student of Crates of Thebes, one of the most prominent cynical philosophers of all time, was the founder of the notion of Stoicism, and in around 300 B.C. introduced the notion to Athens which at the time was a hub of philosophical discourse.

The school of thought was named 'Stoicism' after the Greek words 'Stoa' and 'Poikile' which were used to refer to the painted Athenian porches from which Zeno of Citium was known to preach.

The Stoic philosophy, as it developed, was built on the correlation of three major tenants – Physics, Logic, and Ethics, the combination of which was thought to help a person attain *eudaimonia* a state of successful happiness or contentment.

The **physics** of Stoicism was simple – all things are tangible, and there is nothing that is not tangible, not God, not logic, or reason, not even thoughts or emotions – their logic was that the concept of a separation of heaven and earth was as impossible as the separation of the body and soul. At the same time, the Stoics promoted the notion of *pneuma* or spirit, which they believed acted as the fuel of all things. This was closely linked with the notion of **logic**, which in Stoicism was thought to stem from verbosity. The idea is that each individual word had a tangible existence, which when spoken in a sentence was what crafted all of the cognitive experiences that a person would have and use to develop their persona and basic behavioral reactions. It was here that the concept of **ethics** would come into play – unlike cynics who deemed human construct such as laws, societies or cultures to be artificial and distinct from nature, Stoics took a much more lax view on the matter and encouraged life in accordance with laws and customs, claiming that such social and communal thoughts in themselves were extensions of nature.

The easiest way to understand this is by looking at Diogenes, the famous Greek philosopher, who was known not only for sassing Alexander the Great but also for eating, masturbating, and even defecating in public – now, Diogenes, a cynic, viewed this as the only way to truly divest oneself of worldly desires. Frankly, that isn't something that would help in modern day to day life and that is where Stoicism comes in. Stoicism is a more mellow form of cynicism, it's not telling you to go thumb your finger at all social norms and laws, but rather teaches followers to accept the world around them, make peace with it, and then to seek virtue and happiness.

Pretty intense, isn't it?

But how does this impact us and why is Stoicism so important in the 21st century?

Take a minute – think of the choices you've been making recently, the discussions you've had, and the fights you've been in. Think of all of those extra emotions; rage, anger, happiness, disappointment, and how often they have to lead you to make a decision.

Now, re-evaluate how often these choices have been the right choices.

In our attempt to balance the 'natural world' with the world we live in, we are often prone to deviation – that is to say, we tend to get distracted and end up doing things that aren't logically what is the best choice.

Some people call this following their heart but in truth, it is following an impulse, and the thing about impulses, is the unlike instinct – impulses are reactions to our surroundings which means we are not doing what's best, we are doing what external circumstances make us think we should.

You're essentially being lead around with an imaginary noose.

So, how do you stop letting your emotions rule you?

Hello, Stoicism!

We're not going to be going into a play by play just yet though. First, you need to understand how and why Stoicism came about so that you can then start to explore how to include Stoicism into your own life.

Let's start with the people who are the face of Stoicism, so that you can understand how and where the entire concept stems from, as well as how history's greatest Stoics applied Stoic principles.

Zeno of Citium

Born in 334 B.C. on the island of Cyprus, Zeno of Citium is considered by many to be the Father of Stoicism. Born to Mnaseas, a Phoenician businessman, and a businessman himself Zeno seemed as if he would lead an atypical Greek life. But even as a merchant, Zeno had felt an intense need to be successful. In an effort to find out what he could do to better himself, he sought counsel with an oracle, who told him to 'take on the complexion of the dead'. After having thought about the statement, Zeno took it to mean that he was being told to study ancient authors or scholars and proceeded to do so.

Interestingly, just as he turned thirty, Zeno was shipwrecked on a journey from Phoenicia to Peiraeus. Stranded off the coast of Greece, Zeno began to walk around and soon found himself in an Athenian bookstore. There he came across Xenophon's *Memorabilia*, which held a collection of Socratic writings compiled by one of his students.

Zeno was enthralled and found himself asking the shopkeeper where he could find a man like Socrates, and as luck would have it Crates of Thebes was passing by at that very moment.

The shopkeeper pointed to Crates and Zeno, from that moment on, became his pupil. Crates of Thebes was a cynic and for Zeno, who was from a relatively more conservative upbringing, these teachings were often too 'shameless' for him to emulate. From this, Zeno's Stoicism was born.

Stoicism, for Zeno, meant conforming to the divine or natural way of things and as such, Stoicism is said to lead to true happiness or content. Zeno went on to live in accordance with what was natural or what nature destined. So much so, that later on in 262 B.C., when he one day tripped and fell as he left his school he took this to mean that nature intended for him to die and promptly strangled himself to death.

Slightly misguided, we admit, but hold on for a minute and imagine how liberating it must be to literally want for nothing, the way he did. Zeno feared nothing, not even death and as such nothing controlled him, nothing held him back – can you claim the same?

Seneca

But, there is more, Stoicism did not die with Zeno, in fact, it flourished – even in Rome itself. Here in the hands of Seneca the Younger, or as you may better know him Nero's mentor, came in as a Roman Stoic. He not only lived and embodied affluent Stoicism, but he also worked extensively on developing the more humane sides of Stoic philosophy, as the relationship between Stoicism and compassion, or self-

14

awareness. Even though his own life was rife with drama, the man had an affair with Nero's sister, after all, Seneca wrote and studied Stoicism almost in its exclusivity. This fact made him one of the most influential Stoics of all time, influencing Francis Bacon, Pascal, and even Erasmus. Pretty impressive, eh?

Gaius Musonius Rufus

The real 'Roman Socrates' however, wasn't Seneca but Rufus. Unlike his predecessor who was the topic of much scrutiny for the hypocritical bent of his own wealth and choices, Rufus was the Stoic to live up to, with his life mirroring his philosophy perfectly. Interestingly, it wasn't Rufus who made it to the list of the top three Stoic philosophers of his time but his student Epictetus.

However, regardless of that, Rufus was and will remain perhaps the most perfect Stoic in history. He did not let anything waver his stance, not even his own fear or ego. Where other Stoics when banished, chose death over banishment to ease their pride. Musonius Rufus boldly asked, *"If you choose death because it is the greater evil, what sense is there in that? Or if you choose it as the lesser-evil, remember who gave you the choice. Why not try coming to terms with what you have been given?"*. It was for these reasons that he was and continues to be so revered. Like Muddy Waters to the Rolling Stones, Musonius stood out and inspired the most iconic Stoics of history, and his worth and value was visible and stood out to those who knew what to value.

Epictetus

Of all of the Stoic scholars, one of the reasons Epictetus stands out was because of his sheer perseverance. Born as a slave to a wealthy household in modern-day Turkey, Epictetus studied under Musonius Rufus. Soon after the death of Emperor Nero, he became a freeman who taught all that he had learned to the Roman masses for a quarter-century until Rome banished philosophers entirely.

Unlike his mentor, who prized ethics above almost everything, Epictetus was known for having a religious tone to his teachings. Even going on to state, 'God has entrusted me with myself,' and it is this that made Stoicism so popular among many Christian scholars, who found his two maxims preaching acceptance of events which were directed by a higher power to be appealing and in line with their own beliefs.

Marcus Aurelius

And finally, the legendary Roman Emperor, Marcus Aurelius is our last Stoic on the list. With his book *Meditations* being one of the most read books of all time and almost religiously studied by numerous world leaders and iconic successes, such as Bill Clinton and J. K. Rowling. Marcus' own take on Stoic philosophy had much to do with endurance and was what many believe to be a primitive form of cognitive behavior therapy – in fact, the emperor was known not only for his fortitude but also for his immense strength of mind. Yet despite all of this, Marcus was an extremely compassionate leader, his ability to navigate the emotional pull of sorrow and joy flawlessly despite the intense pressure he faced as an emperor and a warrior was and remain a commendable feat. Perhaps his most base lesson being that it was important that people as individuals learn how to be happy with who they were, and more importantly, that they accepted and cherish themselves to the point where they were not longing to be someone else. At the same time, it was equally important that people did not love their lives so much that they were in constant fear of losing it, while the conversely shouldn't be so hurt and troubled by it that they choose to end it. In a word, he preached and practiced fortitude, and so much of it that he remains to this day an icon of it.

Now, that's a pretty deep dive am I right?

But other than learning about a bunch of old guys, what are we taking away from this?

Context.

We're taking the context and adding that into our understanding of Stoic practicalities. What understanding, you may ask – the one you're about to get!

The Three Practicalities of Stoicism

Stoic philosophy isn't just about a bunch of old dudes being virtuous. It's actually deeply rooted in the concepts of happiness and contentment in human lifetimes and how a specific set of practices can help people find peace, despite any circumstantial issues that may arise. In short, it's a cheat code for the human race, a way for us to find joy without having to fight and claw for it.

So, what are the three most important lessons that we are about to take from Stoicism and implement directly into our own lives?

Why don't you keep reading to find out?

1. Time is Treasure –

Despite time being the most precious of commodities, we have a tendency to not only give time away freely but also to somehow disregard its value. We tend to think that there will always be a tomorrow waiting, to do all the good things or all the important things and as we do this; we lose today, tomorrow, and all our tomorrows.

As Stoic philosopher Marcus Aurelius says, *'Don't behave as if you are destined to live forever. What's fated hangs over you. As long as you live and while you can, become good. Now.'* Or as we say now, stop procrastinating!

2. Controlling Your Feelings –

The one thing that Stoicism is perhaps best known for, is controlling emotions. While it is often mistakenly thought to mean that one should erase their emotions. In reality, the Stoic focus is on three things – *apatheia, ataraxis,* and *autarkeis. Apatheia* is the ability to be free from emotional constraints such as pain, anxiety, or suffering and, on the other hand, *autarkeis* is the ability to conserve this freedom and to ensure that it sustains. *Ataraxis,* on the other hand, is a state of being usually encountered when *apatheia* and *auarkeis* are achieved. Here, your emotions themselves become fortified so that they cannot be wavered by external feelings such as fear or stress.

As the Roman Emperor says,

'Choose not to be harmed – and you won't feel harmed. Don't feel harmed – and you haven't' been.'

3. Be Virtuous –

You'll find that throughout this book, at numerous points, we talk about making choices that are right or choices that are virtuous. This is because virtue or the pursuit of goodness is a

19

core tenant of the subject. As we move forward with life, we tend to see the same; life is worthy when you do what is right. The one thing we should prioritize above all others is goodness; such as honesty over lies, modesty over shamefulness, and values over hypocrisy.

Understanding the Book You Hold

Now, all this must seem like it's pretty heavy reading – and what are you supposed to do with all of this information anyway, right?

Well, as for what you're supposed to do with it – that's simple, you're expected to use it just as Warren Buffet, Bill Clinton, Elon Musk, and Jeff Bezos have, to develop their lives and their companies into something bigger than themselves.
How you're supposed to do so is pretty simple too!

Start by going through every Chapter one at a time. As you come to the end of each chapter, take a week off and try to apply all that you have learned from the chapter in your actual day to day dealings. Practice each lesson until it becomes second nature. Remember Stoicism is a lifestyle, not a fad.

If all goes well, seven Chapters and seven weeks later, you will not only find an amazing sense of balance and peace in your life – you'll also be able to use that balance to promote positivity in the things you do and develop a more productive lifestyle.

So, what do you think? Are you ready to become the best version of yourself?

Chapter 1: Introspection: Know Thyself

'Look within. Within is a fountain of good,
and it will ever bubble up if thou wilt ever
dig.' – Marcus Aurelius

If there is one major curse that our generation is besieged with, it would be the senseless FOMO trend that seems to have captivated all of us. Long gone are the days when one would take the time to look at or even maybe deliberate on one's actions – instead nowadays our emotions and memories dictate our actions.

Why did we do something? Because we *felt* like it.

That in itself is possibly the most childish approach to life in existence. Yet for years, we have been justifying it claiming we don't know which day is our last and that we need to live for the moment.

But, what we never asked ourselves was, why does what we feel have to be at odds with what is right?

Why can't we want what is right?

And if we aren't longing for what is 'right' – why aren't we?

What is biasing us, what is controlling us and worse, what is influencing us, without us realizing?

These are the questions we as a generation have forgotten how to ask, and worse, the same questions we have failed to answer.

But it's never too late to begin.

Take a minute.

Think back to the quote we started with.

'Look within'.

Ask yourself, why does Stoicism encourage us to look within? Why are we encouraged to understand ourselves? The answer is in the very next line, 'within is a fountain of good and it will ever bubble up if thou wilt ever dig.'

Because at our core, we are good. We are prudent, we are just, we have the fortitude, and we are temperate. Stoicism knows this, Stoicism just wants you to recognize it for yourself, within yourself.

Do you think you're ready to understand why it's so important and how you can practice it?

Well, to do so – the first thing you need to understand is that true introspection is based on four fundamental principles – Self-Esteem, Self Confidence, Self-Awareness, and Emotional Control. Now, while we will go into each of the principles in depth, in a moment, let's first focus on the commonalities and differences of the four.

Self Esteem and Self Confidence, for instance, are often seen to be interchangeable. We claim that one lacks confidence or self-esteem – what then is the difference? Simply put, self-esteem is the perception you have of your own being, who you are, how you feel about yourself, and what value do you put upon yourself. In short – what are you worth, in your own eyes?

Self Confidence, on the other hand, is different. Here you are dealing with another weighing in of sorts, not on yourself but rather on a certain skill at a certain time, this is why self-confidence is so subjective. While you may not be very confident about your cooking skills, you could be super confident about how well you speak or play the guitar. It is, as you can see, entirely dependent on the situation and the context in which your skill is being judged.

Self-Awareness is similar but a bit more distinct. whereas, Self Confidence and Self- Esteem deal with your biased perception of your own strengths or weaknesses, Self-Awareness, on the other hand, deals with the same things but in an unbiased way. Who you are, what you are seen to be by your peers, or (if you're dealing with businesses) who you come off as to clients or prospective employees, is key.

Emotional Control, however, is the only clearly distinct issue you'll find yourself confronting – which is interesting because it is also arguably the most important. Whereas, the trifecta of Self-Esteem, Self-Confidence, and Self-Awareness seem to be dealing with your notion of self and the various perceptions of it. Emotional Control is like the key to the lock, it opens up the issue of why and how your perceptions come about and what you can do to liberate them from petty matters such as pride or fear.

Sounds pretty intense, doesn't it? Time to hit the ground running!

Remember, you've got this.

Take a deep breath, steady yourself, and here we go!

Self-Esteem

> *'Everything we hear is an opinion, not a fact.*
> *Everything we see is a perspective, not the*
> *truth.' – Marcus Aurelius*

You are the sum of your thoughts.

That is to say, everything you choose to hear and choose to see is based on how you choose to see the world. Or rather how your self-esteem has allowed you to. As Marcus Aurelius says, all that we hear is in truth an opinion and all that we see is simply one side of the story, one perspective, a perspective which stems from our biased view of the world as opposed to the actual facts of the matter.

You see, your self-esteem is part of a cycle – you are the sum of your thoughts.

If we see ourselves as valuable, we then value our time and what we do with it, which in turn means we try to engage in activities that have value and add value. Whereas, if we fail to see the worth in ourselves, we continue down that spiral by not valuing our time or our actions, and so it goes on.

This is where Stoicism comes in, Stoics realize that self-esteem is a state of mind, as opposed to a universal truth. In fact, one of Stoicism core tenants is to act on logic or ethics as opposed to emotion or feeling. Which is why it is critical to Stoic principles for one to be able to build a sense of self that is distinct from their judgment and perception of specific events. Stoicism, therefore, preaches a more tolerant positive approach to thought processing, almost as if we are using a form of mental and emotional hygiene to cleanse our perception.

So, what then, are the ABC's of Self-Esteem? Three things -

1. Controlled Judgement
2. Positive Productivity and
3. Self-Dependency

Controlled judgment is the central issue here, after all, it is your judgment of a situation that sets the tone for how your mind will perceive it. It is here that we need to start to introduce a more compassionate, as opposed to a more critical, view of self. When we are upset with ourselves, when we consider ourselves to have underperformed, or feel like we haven't lived up to the expectations we had of ourselves we begin to launch into a critical self-monologue. For many this is a defense mechanism, we say ugly, horrible things in the hopes that others will see that we are already chastising ourselves and will refrain from doing so themselves. While hoping that our own criticisms will help us build a thicker skin, and as such protect us from other people and what they will think or say. For others though, self-critique is a default mechanism if something has gone wrong, we must have done something to cause it, we are quick to assign and accept blame because we see explanations to be weaknesses and we are afraid of weakness above all.

So, what is the alternate option – what can we do instead of giving in to this negative landslide? Meet – Self-Compassion.

Despite the fact that we often give ourselves a hefty dose of criticism or judgment, much more than what we would deliver upon any random passerby, we oddly seem to find it hard to give ourselves even an ounce of the same compassion that we would afford even to a stranger. Odd, isn't it?

Let's change that – or at the least let's take conscious steps to try to.

So, what do we do? Let's start by having you teach yourself that it is okay to be imperfect, in fact, every time you pick out a flaw in yourself, balance it out by naming something you love about yourself. This positive balance will force you to acknowledge that there is more good to you than you care to admit. And this is the next step, stop feeling shame in admitting the good things about yourself, remember embarrassment is not a Stoic characteristic.

Don't believe it?

Remember Zeno of Citium? Yeah, the founder of Stoicism. Well, do you remember how we mentioned that his first mentor was Crates of Thebes? Crates of Theebes was a notorious cynic, in fact, he was well known for throwing off many of the social norms associated with 'civilized society'. He would eat, defecate, and even masturbate in public – all of which were considered severe breaches of decorum in ancient Greece. Now, Zeno was never really able to fully adopt Crates' shamelessness, he grew up on a small island off the coast of Cyprus, and had a more conservative upbringing that Crates, or even than most other Athenians. Crates recognized this in Zeno, and to him, it was a flaw. His logic was simple, if you feel enough to feel shame or embarrassment for your own harmless actions, you are not distancing yourself from man's artificial constructs of society well enough. And as such he decided to teach young Zeno a lesson. Crates gave Zeno a pot of lentil soup to carry through the town, embarrassed Zeno attempted to hide and disguise the pot as he carried it. As carrying food through open spaces such as Crates had bidden was considered unseemly. Crates refused to allow Zeno to wallow in self-pity, which stemmed from self-shame and struck the pot with a stick so that the pot broke and the soup covered Zeno, forcing Zeno to now continue with food all over his being and not just himself.

The lesson Crates had sought to teach Zeno was simple – embarrassment is a useless emotion and only serves to keep you from properly completing your task. Today, you need to learn the same. Allowing shame to build in you, so that it can be used to control you with negativity is unproductive. Instead of constantly shaming yourself and critiquing yourself, afford yourself the courtesy of kindness just as you would a small child – you will find that a positive sense of self, in the long run, is much better than living with a person you detest.

This brings us to Positive Productivity, a major reason why we lack self-esteem or why we end up losing it, is because we keep on biting off more than we can handle. Taking on tasks that are beyond our ability and then faulting ourselves for not being able to keep up is a major issue. Instead, try to focus on tasks that you do well and slowly build on those skills.

It's important to be able to identify your true skills here because often we go after things we are just not meant to do. Even if you are trained to be an accountant if you don't have an affinity for numbers your job may be burdensome and hard to excel in. Find your true calling by experimenting with what works for you, the better you are able to understand your own skills and weaknesses the better you will be able to build a strong business foundation. Remember, you are not defined by your weaknesses. You are defined by your choices and that is why perception is so important.

When asked what advice they would want to impart on their younger selves, if they could go back in time, billionaire influencers such as Bill Gates and Mark Zuckerberg both talked about the perception of 'intelligence' and how there is no 'right' way to be smart. Because society has imprinted on our minds that intelligence is a one-dimensional subject that can be measured by specific metrics such as IQ tests, we have a tendency to hold a variety of people and minds to the same standard.

Einstein once famously said that everyone is a genius, but if we judged fish by how well they climbed trees we'd always believe them to be stupid. Keep this in mind when you're struggling with your self-esteem and instead of allowing negativity to flood your mind, try to face your self-esteem issues head-on.

If your self-esteem is tattered, work on it. Be self-dependent. If you have a weakness, don't' expect to be magically good at it one fine morning, try to fix it and at the same time try to see if there is a better alternative for you. It may take time and it will most definitely take patience, but to be able to persevere against the odds is a key component of true Stoicism.

So, keep your chin up, and keep going!

Self-Confidence

'You can tell the character of every man when you see how he gives and receives praise.' – Seneca

As you slowly start to rebuild your sense of self, you will soon find that you also need to start working on how you perceive your abilities. After all, it isn't always just ourselves that we pass harsh judgments on, our skills and talents go through the same unfortunate process. Stoic philosophy knows this and points it out, as does Seneca, as he talks about how people react to praise, noting that our dependence on it is what defines our own self-confidence. We speak as we fear we are viewed and we accept the views that we think we deserve, as such our own judgment of what we are worth, and what we are capable of is critical, to our understanding of self.

So, how do we move forward?

To begin, you'll need to first recognize the power of your thoughts. You see, your thoughts are more than your view or perception of any one thing, they are what set the tone for every thought you will have thereafter and how you will perceive every action you see. If you continue to tell yourself that you are 'worthless' or 'beyond saving', your actions slowly start to reflect those notions. So, watch not just what you say, but also how you think. Remember, compassion trumps cruelty.

The next thing you need to remember to do is to be focused. Remember, confidence is built on actions. So, in order to be able to truly be confident in your own abilities, you need to work on having a plan – in truth though, in terms of modern-day businesses we seem to be drowning in plans. We call for a meeting after meeting and console ourselves with the thought we are making plans and taking actions – but when asked what actions we have taken, the answer is that we've planned to take action. It's like a dog chasing his tail.

We keep going round and round in circles, not realizing that we need to break away and move forward in order to truly achieve anything. Stop.

Billionaire Bill Gates once famously said that if there was one thing that helped him build Microsoft, it was the fact that from a very young age he had confidence in his own self and his abilities. Confidence gives you courage, and it is this courage that later becomes the fuel you burn when you work on overcoming obstacles and going further in life.

When Gates and his college friend Paul Allen, first reached out to the maker of Altair claiming they had a programming language that could run on their computers, they didn't even have an Altair to test it on much less an actual language – but they were confident they could make it. And when Altair's president asked to see them, they spent weeks creating the language which they typed into Altair's own computer system in Albuquerque for the first time – and like magic, it worked.

What guarantees did they have? None.

What got them through? Confidence.

What use are plans or genius ideas if you don't do anything to achieve them. At a point, your actions are all that matter. So, if you want to get away from a bad boss and try your hand at writing that novel you think could be the next *Harry Potter*, what use is it to talk about it if you haven't done anything. Stop thinking, stop planning, just do what you've been saying you will do. Your actions will speak louder than any 'research' or 'preparation' – so stop planning, take hold of your thoughts, take responsibility for them and just get up and act.

Now, as we move forward with our actions, you'll find that our successes are often tempered by failures.

We make mistakes.

We do things wrong.

We all do – none of us are perfect, and that's fine, failure is inevitable when it comes to life. The true test of our character is what we choose to do with our failures.

For most people, failures are the end of the line. We fail and then we run away as if running far enough or fast enough will keep our failures from staining our pride. We forget, rather conveniently, that failure is part of the learning process. Our ability to do something right stems from our ability to accept failure, and even look forward to it. As Thomas Alva Edison once famously said, 'I have not failed 10,000 times. I have successfully found 10,000 ways that will not work.'. The ability to look beyond failure and to allow it to simply pass you by, as opposed to allowing it to define you, is a critical part of Stoicism. Take this opportunity to think back on a recent mistake you have made, and ask yourself – what did you learn from it?

Once you determine what it is you have learned, say thank you. It may sound like an odd thing to do, but thankfulness is actually one of the most important building blocks when it comes to self-confidence. By being thankful, you are acknowledging the good in another person, or at times yourself, and this acknowledgment helps you promote positive thinking. A famous South Korean Pop Band, by the name BTS, recently began taking over music charts in the US. During one of their initial visits, an American passerby called out to the band telling them they would never make it in America. A year later, they were AMA winning, Grammy nominees taking over the world.

Any idea what Jung Hoseok, the band member who heard, said in response? 'Thank you for your concern.' Not only did his acknowledgment take away any power the words were intended to have over the band, but his response by focusing on the good, allowed him to sidestep all the negativity the words would have carried with them.

So, the next time someone says something to you that is designed to perhaps undercut your confidence, take the sting out of it and find a way to be thankful for it.

And the final bit?

Expectations.

If there is one silent enemy that our self-confidence has a tough time facing head-on, it is an expectation. What are expectations though? Is it an expectation to assume you'll do well on a test that you studied for, or that you'd get a promotion you worked hard for? Well, to be honest – both are. Now, I know what you're thinking, but how is that fair, I worked hard for those things and they are what I deserve.

That very thought right there is an expectation. The entitlement you have for the future and its effect on your present. Now, Stoicism isn't telling you to just suck it up all the time, Stoicism is about action, remember. When something wrong is happening, address it – make a plan and act on it. But when it comes to the little things, the things that are ruining your present, like you worrying about a long term relationship with a person you literally just matched with on Tinder – yeah, those have got to go. As Gates says, try new things, this allows you to find out what works for you and what doesn't, as opposed to just sitting around and making assumptions.

Don't daydream about things that may or may not ever happen – focus on the task at hand, not only will this help you be more productive, but it'll also keep you from allowing your confidence to fade in the face of trials and tribulations that may never come to pass. Remember, when you transform your ability to be a strong, productive member of society, you are in turn adding value to your skills and helping boost your confidence.

Self-Awareness

> 'These reasonings are unconnected: "I am richer than you, therefore I am better"; "I am more eloquent than you, therefore I am better." The connection is rather this: "I am richer than you, therefore my property is greater than yours" But you, after all, are neither property nor style.' – Epictetus

Self-Awareness is the last of the self-imposed measures poised to not only determine but help grow a clearer sense of self. The concept of self-awareness is actually a very common soft-skill taught around the world to business leaders and business graduates – understand who you are in isolation and work towards improving yourself.

The concept, however, was coined first by Stoic philosophers such as Epictetus and Marcus Aurelius who encouraged people to view themselves separately from what they had in terms of material riches, or what they had achieved in terms of power or success.

The real question is who you are and whether or not *you* are being the best possible version of yourself both internally and externally.

In truth, there is no one better placed to properly test out if you are living up to your potential and principles, then you are. Epictetus used to use a specific word '*dokimazo*' – to refer to this testing. He would encourage, as did many philosophers before him, that you brutally test your own perceptions and opinions, and that you do the opposite for others or rather seek to see the best in them.

There were two reasons for this – one was to avoid self-deception, which was viewed to be a disease like in nature and would prevent self-growth and learning. The other was to promote positive thinking and at the same time to keep us from thinking too highly of ourselves.

Self-awareness is critical when dealing with businesses and business choices, not just because it gives you a more realistic view of what's going on- but also because it ensures that you are more in tune with your own inner voice. Billionaires such as tech giant Steve Jobs and media mogul Oprah Winfrey have both discussed this at length.

Oprah Winfrey, who was once an upcoming journalist demoted from co-anchor position and later went on to host the highest-rated talk show in Chicago for over 25 years, explains that unless one takes the time to actually know who they are and why they are here, they will continue to struggle.

In her own words, 'I've come to believe that each of us has a personal calling that's as unique as a fingerprint – and that the best way to succeed is to discover what you love and then find a way to offer it to others in the form of service, working hard, and also allowing the energy of the universe to lead you.'

So, before you move on to do anything else – stop.

Figure out what it is that you want to achieve in life.

Who do you want to be?

What works for you?

What is it that you love?

How can you give this to others?

Once you've got that down pat – we can move on to the last level of introspection.

Ready?

Emotional Control

'It does not matter what you bear, but how you bear it.' - Seneca

Emotional control is the key to any fruitful application of self-applied introspection. Imagine you have evaluated your self-confidence, your self-esteem, and your self-awareness – none of this will amount to anything if while doing your testing or evaluating you were biased, or if after testing you were biased towards the results.

Now, generally speaking, Stoicism in its 'common' definition is thought to refer to the expulsion of all emotional or passion-driven reactions that swell up within our consciousness. This, however, is not the case, Stoics have never advocated the suppression of emotions. They have merely sought for individuals to cultivate such consciousness that they can control the manner in which such emotions arise so that they can better avoid negative emotions and bask in the positive ones.

The term 'emotional control' itself is a bit tricky – it seems to suggest that we would be able to control our emotions before they arise, and control them in a manner that only some would come forth, but in actuality what you are doing is controlling them *as* they come forth. Your emotions are what you feel and while, like fear when in a life or death situation, you can't control that emotion coming forward, you can control how you act in regard to that emotion. Hence, Seneca claiming that what you bear isn't important, instead of how you bear it is of more consequence.

This is because as a rule when you are reacting, your reactions are to another person's action and to a certain extent are senseless and ergo outside of your control. This lack of control is the problem.

So how do you cultivate emotional control?

Well, for most professionals the rule is to play poker. You see, in order to succeed in poker, a critical rule is to respond and not react to the cards you are dealt with. Much like life, you have little to no control over what you are dealing with and there is no logic or reason to the events that can and will surround you.

The trick here is to follow four cardinal rules. School your mind to understand these four things, to believe in them, and to apply them and you are set to face the world.

The first rule is that 'There is No Perfection'. As a human, the life that you live is outside your control. Even in the things that are in your control, there will always be things that escape you, these things in layman terms are called 'mistakes' and are a natural, inevitable part of life. You will never be perfect, nothing you ever do will be perfect. There will always be room for improvement and there will always be a better way, that is okay. Accept this as a part of life and move on instead of wallowing in self-pity. There are bigger things to focus on. So, do it.

The second rule of thumb is that you must 'Say No to Temptation' – as you move forward with ideas or projects it's very easy to get side-tracked by something that seems like a newer, shinier object. Stay true to your goal, understand that all that glitters is not gold and that willpower is an important component of Stoic success. While a steady 9-5 job may seem to appeal to you over a small startup, know that if you have started something you owe it to the project to see it through; do not waver and do not falter. If you don't work for your own dreams now, you will work to serve another's dreams forever – so which is it going to be?

Thirdly 'Say No to Messes' – no matter what you do, you need to ensure that you are not only being strategic and organized, you must also be transparent and tactical so that you can curb your impulses and follow the plan, as opposed to jumping the gun on a hunch. Remember your instincts are good, but your clarity of mind is better.

Which of course brings us to the final factor, 'Say No to What Ifs' – one of the biggest threats to emotional stability is the notion of 'what if' – not only do statements like this aggravate the mind and trigger despair and stress, they result in the loss of valuable time and resources. Don't waste your time on if's, but's, or maybe's work on what you have, with what you have and you'll actually achieve *something*.

Chapter 2: Productivity

'If a person doesn't know to which port they sail, no wind is favorable.' – Seneca

One of the core tenants of Stoic philosophy is the constant issuance of mental self-awareness reminders. Imagine if every time you did something, there was an actual voice in your head that holds you accountable.

What are you doing?

Who are you doing it for?

Is it virtuous?

Is it in line with the natural order of justice?

By holding your mind accountable, Stoicism as a practice forces people to reflect daily on their thoughts and actions. By curating your actions and thoughts so that all of your actions come from purposed thoughts, you find yourself creating physiological programming of sorts where your brain hardwires you to both commits to and expect achievement. You are basically talking yourself into being 'efficient' and 'productive' in your thoughts and actions, which just happen to be the two most important words in the Stoic dictionary.

By forcing individuals to create mental roadmaps to deal with issues, Stoicism allows people to bypass the 'niceties' of polite society and move ahead and deal with the actual happenings.

It sounds like something we all need in our lives, doesn't it?

Why don't we simplify it a bit for you and help you figure out exactly how to be a more productive, efficient, and balanced person; both in your personal and professional life?

Sound good?

Awesome!

Here we go!

Actions versus Doubts

'Progress daily in your own uncertainty. Live in awareness of the questions.' – Bremer Acosta

As we move forward with Stoicism, we will soon find that the central point of any lifestyle is not necessarily the principles that it is built on but rather how those principals are invoked. For Stoicism it is the same, the more eye-catching issue is not necessarily what Stoicism is about but rather, how it impacts our actions.

Any form of action, even inaction itself, stems from a decision. You have decided to act. Or alternatively, you have decided not to act.

This form of decision-making when in the hands of a Stoic comes across a series of questions. Before we go into them however, let's quickly review what Stoic principles teach us – in Stoicism the one thing that supersedes all others is a virtue. The ultimate goal of Stoicism is after all to be a virtuous being. So, does that mean you get to recklessly do whatever you want in the name of looking out for the greater good? Like if you turned down a well-paying job at a cigarette company because cigarettes are harmful when you have young children to feed and clothe.

No.

Stoicism may be based on virtue, but it also holds you accountable for your actions.

So how do you know, when you are supposed to act and when you are supposed to restrain yourself?

Start by asking yourself a question, as Acosta says, you must live in awareness of the questions. Ask yourself, is the matter at hand in your control?

If it is not, there is no point in you fussing or worrying about it, as there is nothing you can do to change it. For instance, if you are dealing with an important tender and you know that there is going to be a critical 2nd bidder making a bid today, is it helpful for you to go into a panic and worry about it? Will your worrying about it cause the second bidder not to bid? No! And as such, any action undertaken at this moment is pointless and should mean nothing to you.

On the other hand, if you are perhaps partially in control, it is important for you to then distinguish over which part of the matter is within your control – the effort or the outcome. If the outcome is not within your control, stop fussing about it and again recognize that this is not your concern. If it is, you would deal with it in accordance with Stoic virtues.

If on the other hand, only the attempt is under your control, you must focus on the attempt and as you do so, ask whether the attempt is virtuous. Your colleague Bob is about to be fired, can you stop him from being fired? No. Can you make an attempt? Yes, but then you must ask of the attempt is virtuous – is Bob a good worker, did he have a valid reason for doing whatever he did? If he did, trying to save his job would be virtuous or good and you as a Stoic should take actions to help in the interest of wisdom, justice, and temperance. If he isn't though, and trying to save his job would be in conflict with those principles, taking actions would not be preferred.

So, all you really have to do is ask yourself a few questions, but as Bremer says, you also need to be aware of your uncertainty so that you *do* ask the questions.

The problem when it comes to the applicability of these factors, however, is that human beings don't react well to change, so we don't know what to do with uncertainty. In fact, the doubt-avoidance tendency that is second nature to us has been at the forefront of many corporate failures. Billionaire Charlie Munger, who was Warren Buffett's right-hand man, has described the situation by explaining how hard the brain works to avoid working to learn something new, which to us are presented in the form of doubts. The solution as advocated by Munger is to cultivate *worldly wisdom*, something that he refers to as a form of multi-disciplinary knowledge that helps approach understanding on a whole as part of a more cohesive framework, kind of like understanding that a business is dependent on both people and systems and that both channels have different reactions, different foundations and as such must be dealt with in different manners.

Make sense?

Productivity

'If you accomplish something good with hard work, the labor passes quickly, but the good endures; if you do something shameful in pursuit of pleasure, the pleasure passes quickly, but the shame endures.' – Gaius Musonius Rufus

As we move on to the element of productivity in its micro sense, you will find that you are faced not only with a large never-ending list of to-do's, you are also faced with limited time and somehow the two don't quite add up.

Now, before we start worrying about the imbalance in terms of your time and work ratio (we'll get to that in just a minute, don't worry!), why don't we take a moment to look a little closer at the 'tasks' or jobs you need to get through to be productive – because that's what productivity is all about right? Getting more done in less time?

Buzz!

Nope. Wrong answer!

Productivity in Stoicism is underpinned by two things. One the value or worth of the task, as we discussed earlier – does the task have value in virtue, if yes than it is an appropriate task, if not, it is not.

On the other hand, the importance of the task and its balance against urgency is also super important and is a great way to figure out what is actually necessary. So, who used to use these methods, try Eisenhower, yup, *that* Eisenhower, POTUS 34, the man behind NASA, and the internet and all of that fancy stuff.

So how did he do it?

Eisenhower used to use something he referred to as the box, basically, it was his way of using Stoic principles to sort through the stuff he needed to do. There were four major categories; Important, Not Important, Urgent, and Not Urgent. When it came to deciding what he had to do, POTUS 34 would identify which things were both urgent and important, aka they had virtue, and got to them straight away. As Musonius Rufus, yet another famous Stoic, puts it if you are doing something good by working hard, it may have required a little powering through but the benefits continued. As for the stuff that wasn't important or urgent, like scrolling your newsfeed or drawing up a prettier version of your daily routine so that it looks better – Eisenhower would simply scrap them. If it wasn't important and it wasn't urgent, he just wouldn't do it.

What about when something was urgent, as in it had to be done by this week, but it wasn't a super important task? For instance, if you're a lawyer and your case list for the next week needs to be updated, it needs to be done by next week but it doesn't necessarily need a managing partner looking into it – simple, you delegate! Pass the buck on to someone who has less on their plate and give yourself a little room, you'll need it! Especially since, when it comes to non-urgent tasks that *are* important, you need to schedule in some time and get cracking. It may not be something you particularly want to but you need to get it done, so why procrastinate?

All in all, the key to productivity isn't working more or working harder – it's working smarter! Instead of doing a million things, figure out the things you need to do *right now* and do them. Then make a list and schedule in the other things that you need to do ultimately in the future. Everything else that can survive without you, you delegate or you let go completely and just like that your work burden has been halved as have your stress levels!

Now all that's left is for you to do the things that need to be done, in an efficient manner!

Efficiency

> 'So in the majority of other things, we
> address circumstances not in accordance
> with the right assumptions, but mostly by
> following wretched habit.' - Gaius Musonius
> Rufus

While processing through our task list, and filtering out what we need versus what we don't need, is a major part of our workload which we've managed to deal with a little more productively. We won't be productive as a whole if we fail to address the *way* in which we approach these individual tasks.

What are we doing? Why are we doing it? How are we doing it? Is this the best way to do it?

These may seem like simple questions but they are actually super important, not just because they help you re-evaluate how and why you are doing what you are doing, but also because they help you evaluate if the way in which you are getting the task done in the best possible way to do it.

Think about companies like Google and Amazon, efficiency is key here and the only reason they are big, and they are staying big, is because they are constantly adapting to fit the market needs. As a company and an employee, unlike when you are a student, you have to keep in mind that in the real-world, routine and habits actually detract from efficiency. Just think of how much Google has changed and adapted from its early days and how the OG internet browser Explorer seems to have fallen behind – why do you think that is?

Let's be honest, it wasn't like the browser got worse,\ as the years went by, it just didn't get any better and in a constantly evolving world, stagnation is the worst thing that can happen.

If you aren't getting better at your job, you are becoming redundant because somewhere someone is willing to do your job, and for less. Your time has to be an investment that makes you better at what you do, not just something you allow to pass you by.

Which is exactly why it is *so* important to break away from routine. If you feel like what you're doing has become repetitive, that means your mind is settling into a pattern and it's time for you to change things up.

Stop.

Re-evaluate your goal, and then take a hard look at your process – what are you doing, how are you doing it, and what is a better way to achieve the same or better results?

Once you've done that, try adding in those things to your regular routine or better yet throw your routine out altogether and make yourself a new road-map. Remember the goal is to succeed, and sometimes you need to step away from what you know to find another way!

A great tool that you can use, in addition to the Eisenhower Box, is to simply break down your major goals into smaller more manageable goals. So, once you have your final list of the things you need to do, pick any one item off that list and break it down into ten or more tiny tasks that you can get started on. As you go through each of the tasks, tick it off your list. Your mind may be telling you that you haven't done much, but the paper in front of you will testify otherwise. Smaller tasks make larger issues easier to tackle and make them seem less daunting, which helps us get more done!

Pretty cool, eh?

Why don't you grab a piece of paper and break down your task list a little before you move on to the next bit here?

Go on, we'll wait.

Responsibility for the Outcome

> *"The chief task in life is simply this: to identify and separate matters so that I can say clearly to myself which are externals not under my control, and which have to do with the choices I actually control. Where then do I look for good and evil? Not to uncontrollable externals, but within myself to the choices that are my own..."* – *Epictetus*

Okay, so you have your task plan and you know how to go through it in the most effective manner possible – all good things, but say you try and something doesn't go your way.

What do you do now?

Do you wallow in guilt or do you push the blame off on someone else and say it wasn't your fault?

How about – No.

A key principle of Stoicism is the notion of virtue ethics, a direct contrast to the general consequential ethics. The idea is that if you do not have control over the outcome or the results you aren't completely responsible for them. For instance, if your colleague is being ineffective and irresponsible at work and you complain about it and he gets fired – it's not totally your fault.

Now, what about the partial bit though – doesn't that indicate it's our fault a little bit?

Well, when it comes to Stoicism, what it really means is that it *might* be your fault. While generally speaking, outcomes shouldn't be something you worry about but the scenario changes when you are dealing with non-virtuous actions. So why did you complain about your colleague? Were you being malicious? Or were you asked by a superior, as part of your job, to assess the team?

If it's the latter, what you did was a virtuous act and part of your responsibility, and as such, was how you were meant to act. Any subsequent reaction or result of your action, be it positive or negative, has nothing to do with you because you are not in control. You are only in control if you did something out of a malicious intention, where your goal was not virtuous but rather to see your colleague fired.

But that's for others when it comes to yourself the same rules apply.

Stoicism doesn't just mean you have to have a stiff upper lip and pretend nothing affects you. It's more about understanding and being able to distinguish what is in your control and what is outside of it. As Epictetus says in his quote, being able to identify what is in your control and what is beyond your control is important so that you can also understand which acts you actually need to worry about.

Case in point? Your own personal development.

When you take responsibility for yourself, you are in effect shedding any crumbs of a victim mentality. When it comes to your own progress you are not dealing with an external control – you have control and you have the power to decide what will happen to you. Everything that happens to you is something you are allowing to happen.

Why?

Because nature has equipped us with all the necessary tools to deal with life and its obstacles head-on. Stoicism teaches us that in order to improve our chances of leading a happy life, which is the ultimate goal, we have to step up and forcefully take back our own destiny. Have a bad boss? Don't let it ruin your life, be proactive and do something about it. Either go over his head or look actively for another job. Your boss being an ass isn't what is ruining your day, your refusal to take yourself out of that toxic environment is.

Canadian-American CEO and motivational speaker Brian Tracy, has touched upon this issue directly and drawn heavily on Stoic principles as when he talks about superior leaders. In Tracy's opinion, superior leaders are those who are willing to admit to their mistakes and cut their losses instead of stubbornly following through when they know they are dealing with a sinking ship. If you are making a mistake, if you made a mistake, the mistake is not what is going to matter in ten weeks, it's how you dealt with the mistake.

Remember, you are the master of your own fate and as such if you are suffering, *you* are also the one with the solution.

Energy Control

'To achieve freedom and happiness, you need
to grasp this basic truth: some things in life
are under your control, and others are not.
Within your control are your own opinions,
aspirations, desires, and the things that repel
you. We always have a choice about the
content and characters of our inner lives. Not
within your control is literally everything
else. You must remember, that these things
are externals and are none of your concern.'
– Epictetus (Enchiridion)

As we begin to better grasp the basics of Stoicism, we also begin to realize that Stoic productivity relies heavily on efficiency and how we are responsible for certain but not all outcomes. But one thing that a lot of people, particularly in this generation, seem to forget is that not only are we not responsible for the things outside of our control, we also have a duty *not* to worry about them.

Imagine you're a corporate sales manager, in a massive pharmaceutical company, that produces a product called Kanax. Kanax does all the things Xanax does and is a very effective medicine, but it just happens to cost five bucks more than a Xanax. As a sales manager, you have brought up the fact that Kanax isn't likely to be welcomed by consumers and is likely to cause your company a loss, but your boss refuses to listen.

What should you do?

Worry about it, or just do as you're told and try your best to sell the product?

What if I told you, you were asking the wrong question?

Everything you are surrounded with and everything you deal with falls into one of two categories – (a) something you have control over or, (b) something you don't have control over, and both of these are stressors for the mind.

When faced with the former, anxiety or stress can actually cause you to be more ineffective. After all, if you are misusing your energy by worrying over or panicking over an issue, you are in effect wasting time and energy. Worrying about something doesn't change anything, in fact, all it really does is cloud your focus and rob you of clarity of mind and peacefulness. If anything, anxiety, and stress make you make bad choices, like that cigarette you smoke to calm down, or that extra donut you had to cope with all the work stress you're under.

But take a minute and think about it – what have you achieved by being worried? What have you achieved by stressing out? Other than an extra kilo and bad lungs, probably nothing. This is because stressing out or worrying over things you can control basically just keeps you from doing what you need to do. If you *can* do something, do it! Why are you wasting your time worrying, when you can be making a game plan to deal with the issue head-on?

It makes you wonder, doesn't it?

Now, let's take a look at the flip side, if you are dealing with the latter and you don't have control over the issue at hand, your anxiety or stress is again just another way of you wasting your time and energy. This time because no matter how much you worry you can't do anything. Now, if the matter at hand is not something you can influence or impact, how does your worrying about it help?

The solution?

Well, the Stoic solution is to get a grip on your emotions and stop letting them get the better of you. Treat your emotions the way you would children, you humor them but you don't let them run wild. Worry and stress lead to you feeling emotionally drained, tired, and worst of all they tend to suck all the positivity out of you. Instead, be proactive and do something about whatever it is that you are dealing with. Remember doing, not stressing, is what saves the day!

Balance

'When you see anyone weeping for grief,
either that his son has gone abroad or that he

has suffered in his affairs, take care not to be
overcome by the apparent evil, but
discriminate and be ready to say, 'What
hurts this man is not this occurrence itself –
for another man might not be hurt by it – but
the view he chooses to take of it.' As far as
conversation goes, however, do not disdain
to accommodate yourself to him and, if need
be to groan with him. Take heed, however,
not to groan inwardly, too.' – Epictetus
(Enchiridion)

If efficiency and productivity are the two most important words in the Stoic's dictionary, the third most important word must be 'balance'. More often than not, Stoics get a bad rep for being detached or unemotional – but in truth, Stoic philosophy isn't about not being humane or not being emotional, it's about knowing how to draw a line and not cross it.

Ergo, balance.

Stoicism refers to two major forms of balance, one of emotional balance and the other actions. The general idea is that productivity, as a Stoic, would depend on what extent you as an individual are allowing your emotions to fill you and subsequently on how you act on those emotions.

Think of it like this, say you are a doctor who works with Doctors without Borders. You go to Palestine and there, as you are working as a general surgeon, you come across so many hopeless cases that you realize that you are unable to maintain your focus and are sobbing into your pillow every night because there is nothing that you can do to stop the steady influx of literally 'war-torn' victims on your operating table.

This is where you must detach yourself from your emotions internally and move forward. The fact that you care is commendable and an important part of living up to the Stoic principles of compassion and love, but that is for you to express externally perhaps to the loved ones of the victim. But when you are dealing with the victim, if you are envisioning him as a laughing five-year-old with a gap tooth, you aren't going to be able to save their lives – extreme attachment is the exact reason why doctors aren't allowed to operate on their loved ones.

Take the time to understand and feel, but do not allow your feelings to undermine your actions. It helps to realize that what you are doing is important and worthy. Remember Stoicism is, in ways, about catering to something bigger than yourself. As a doctor dealing with patients who are being created by selfish nations playing petty games, you are doing something that makes a difference to those individual lives and that difference is what you are achieving through balance.

When you are following proper Stoic values, your actual ability to do good is amplified. So instead of allowing yourself to be faulted for not being more humane, move to seek more balance, both in your thoughts and your actions, so that you can be both more effective and more productive in what you do.

Time Management

'It is not that we have a short time to live, but that we waste a lot of it.' - Seneca

One of the most important things in Stoic philosophy, that we tend to ignore in real life, is the value of time. Now, oddly enough, we've been taught the value of material things and money almost from our infancy – don't waste food, don't break toys, don't lose your lunch money, you name it.

The logic is always very simple – the things in question are valuable and as such deserve to be treated like the precious commodities they are.

But what about our time?

How often has your time been treated with an inch of the same deference?

You wouldn't go out and randomly start handing random people dollar bills, hell you think twice before dropping spare change in a charity tin, and yet when it comes to your time, you are happy to treat it like we do disposable tissue paper.

Why?

Because, honestly speaking, it's never really occurred to you that your time on earth is limited. Yes, you know that you're going to die at some point in time but you feel like that point of time is so far in the future that it's not something you want to deal with right now, at this given point. In Seneca's words, loss of time came in many different forms, some time was forced away from us, like the endless hours you spend in traffic, other bits have merely slipped away, like the hour your spent-on Facebook earlier, or hour before that when you were procrastinating about something you should have done a week ago.

This is where the importance of time management comes in, Stoics like Seneca, make it clear that time is the most precious of commodities and is to be revered above all other material things. Stoic entrepreneurs feel the same. In fact, multiple billionaires such as Mark Cuban, owner of the Dallas Mavericks and Magnolia Pictures, as well as Apple's Steve Jobs and Twitter CEO Jack Dorsey all take little steps to save time such as cutting out meetings. Mark Cuban has even been noted to state that he never does meetings unless someone is writing a check. Other tactics include avoiding multitasking or having themed days such as the 'No-Meeting Wednesday' trend promoted by Facebook's Dustin Moskovitz.

Whatever you do and however you do it, make a point to remember that a true Stoic makes the most of every little bit of time that they are afforded – and so should you. Be it by planning, apps, personal calendars; make sure that you are using your time in the most efficient manner with the most important people for the things you value the most and which are considered virtuous.

Chapter 3: Motivation and Discipline

"What would have become of Hercules do you think if there had been no lion, no hydra, stag, or boar - and no savage criminals to rid the world of? What would he have done in the absence of such challenges?

Obviously, he would have just rolled over in bed and gone back to sleep. So, by snoring his life away in luxury and comfort he never would have developed into the mighty Hercules.

And even if he had, what good would it have done him? What would have been the use of those arms, that physique, and that noble soul, without crises or conditions to stir him into action?"

The truth of the matter is we aren't all mythological heroes with a greater calling determining our role in life – of course, Hercules had bigger better reasons to be proactive; he was going to save the world multiple times, also the chick he liked was kinda hot.

But why us?

What do we have to look forward to – we're not extraordinary people and we don't lead extraordinary lives. What is so wrong with ordinary people giving in to petty, ordinary luxuries?

Do you really need to drag yourself out of bed to help grow

your little home-brand into a massive conglomerate, just because it has potential? Why can't you just sell newspapers, and busk and be content, right?

Well, for one, we are forgetting that Stoics don't live life by a 'what do I get out of it' policy. As a Stoic, while you are free from the societal expectations of constantly doing more and doing better, you aren't free from the natural rule which is to live life virtuously, meaning you owe a debt to society. If you are growing your economic growth, that's not just beneficial to you, it helps you employ other people in your orbit and help give back to society. It's not about whether you can afford tickets to Cabo, it's about acting to the best of your ability so that you can give Collin, Carol, and Casey a job.

The challenges you face make you who you are. After all, being Stoic about how you control your emotions or how you think isn't going to make you a true Stoic, unless you are also working on your self-discipline and your motivation.

Why?

Because you don't get to pick and choose which Stoic virtues are convenient for you and claim you are being Stoic. Stoicism is a lifestyle, that only works when you take it all in, kind of like a fitness plan.

So, are you ready to take a walk through your steady mental diet for the week?

Here we go!

Motivation

*'Let us prepare our minds as if we'd come to
the very end of life. Let us postpone nothing.
Let us balance life's books each day...The one
who puts the finishing touches on their life
each day is never short of time' – Marcus
Aurelius*

Don't procrastinate.

If one had to sum up everything that Stoicism has preached in
regard to motivation in just two words, those would be the
words.

In the modern world, the whole wave of millennial thoughts
has led to this tendency to prioritize emotions and how we feel
over whatever it is that we need to or should do. Even when it
comes down to something we are supposed to do or something
we need to get done, we wait for 'motivation' or for a divine
feeling that will tell us that we need to or should do whatever
it is we need to do.   •

So how do you get over it?

Simple, you just do.

If you sit around waiting for the right moment or the moment
when you 'feel' like doing whatever you need to do, you may
very well be waiting around forever. Epictetus has a rather
harsh take on this matter and explains in *Discourses* how an
individual suffering from a runny nose has two options - we

can of course easily cry and wail about how we are in agony, or alternatively, we could just wipe our nose and stop looking for an excuse to be upset.

The truth is, you always have a choice.

You *will* always have a choice.

You can choose to act, or you can choose not to.

But what is propelling you to act?

Well, check out for a bit of storytime, yeah?

Once upon a time a court jester by the name Damocles began pandering to his king Dionysius and flattered him claiming that he was a man of wealth and fortune for all that he had. Dionysius, the king, offered to switch places with Damocles so that he would better experience kingship for a day. Ecstatic Damocles agreed and sat comfortably on the throne enjoying all of the luxuries of kingship, however, it all seemed to be tainted by one thing. Dionysius, in his wisdom, had hung a long-unsheathed sword just a hairsbreadth above the throne, so that it would dangle just above Damocles' neck as a way to represent all the anxieties and dangers he faced as a king.

His lesson here was two-fold, on one hand, he is explaining that with great fortune comes great danger and, at the same time in Cicero's studies, it was also a reference to the importance of virtue in life. We all have our own sword of Damocles hanging over our heads. None of us know, when, how, or why we will die and while that is a terrifying thought on its own, it is also a sobering thought.

Everything you do, at every single moment, is a part of the legacy you are about to leave behind.

Think of life as the Truman Show – if everything you are doing is being watched, would you rather be seen to do nothing but laze about like a lump of meat? Or would you rather be a trailblazer, who does everything they put their mind to and open the door for opportunities far and wide both for themselves and others?

You're probably thinking the latter. Now, you may have a little voice in your head that is naysaying this instinct – isn't this simple vanity? – it might ask.

Well, the answer is no. Vanity is a subjective judgment you have placed on action. You perceive this to be vain but the act itself is not vain. Actions on their own do not have weight in terms of attributes, that is to say, they are neither good nor bad nor evil. They simply are.

How then do we know we should do or abstain from action? Simple, we check to ensure it is in alignment with natural principles. Is it good, is it virtuous? If so, it should also be done with haste, in the now. We are not destined to live forever, as Stoicism teaches us again and again. And as such, we have a responsibility to usher in the good and while we still can – that is the only way our life will have meaning.

So, what motivates Stoics? Redundancy.

Our time on earth, and our ability to be something, and do something all hang by an unraveling thread. None of us know when that thread will break, only that it will. So, if you are to be someone worth being, you must be that person now, while you still can.

Discipline

'You must cultivate either your own ruling faculty or externals, and apply yourself either to things within or without you that is, be either a philosophe or one of the vulgar.' –
Epictetus

Now, while motivation to adhere to the Stoic principles or rather the natural principles of life itself can seem hard to come by, there are some things that can make it a little easier on you as a person. The first is the understanding of what you are now seeking. You have developed an understanding of yourself and what is yours by laying the foundations through introspection. You have then used this to cultivate for yourself a course of action that is efficient and balanced and most importantly meets your needs. What you now need is something to get you through your little road map. Something that will give you reason and drive to follow through on your chosen path.

As billionaire co-founder of Groupon Andrew Mason puts it – it isn't being smart but being disciplined that changes the route of success. As Mason describes it, he has on occasion met many people who are more 'traditionally' intelligent than he and who logically, therefore, should be more successful than him.

The reason they aren't is simple, they don't have the self-discipline to be as perseverant as he was, that is to say, they haven't been able to stick to what they should have; and also because they haven't had the self-confidence to see things through.

Ring a bell?

Ever run into a high-school buddy who is doing astoundingly well in life, but literally wasn't half as good as you were in school and wonder what happened?

Well, life happened and by life, we mean the choices you made.

In Mason's own words "I often meet people who seem smarter than me, yet are less capable because they don't have the self-discipline and/or self-confidence to introspect on their ability to do what they think they're going to do and **find ways to iteratively improve**. Amazingly, *it's as simple as that*. It's kind of a sore spot for me because I can't understand why people don't take it more seriously."

So, what do you do? How do you avoid being the type of person Mason seems so peeved about?

And most importantly, how can you be less intelligent and do better? Because let's face it, one of the biggest fears that have consistently held us back year after year has been the fear that we weren't good enough.

Well, start off by forming positive habits, some of the habits that are held by billionaires are actually consciously formed to help promote their productivity and as a result their success.

Start off by focusing on yourself – treat yourself the way you would an expensive blue-chip stock and invest in yourself. Every day, do little things that help you develop, work on learning a new language or make sure you are staying fit. Whatever it is you are doing, make sure you do something for yourself. Why? Because you need to value yourself to be able to discipline yourself. And then next, make sure you are investing time and effort in what you love as well.

Billionaire Elon Musk has talked extensively about having a 100-hour workweek. His logic being that if a person in the same position with the same or higher skills is putting in 40 hours a week and you are putting in some 100 hours a week, you are by default going to be ahead of your competitor by at least one business quarter, which is the very definition of a head start in terms of corporate success – so what are you waiting for?

Perseverance

'To bear trials with a calm mind robs misfortune of its strength and burden.' –
Seneca, Hercules Oetaeus

Have you ever wondered, what it takes, to be successful? According to most millionaires, you're dealing with just two things – persistence and resilience. In Stoic philosophy, Epictetus advocated something similar when he denounced the concept of *cheimaskesai*, or as he defined it part-time soldiering.

What was he referring to?

Before the advent of modern warfare, armies took a winter break when winter actually came about. There was no North waiting in anticipation of war, people simply called a mutual truce until they felt like they were in the mood to go back to battle. Epictetus, believes this concept of taking breaks is extremely detrimental to the achievement of an ultimate goal, his logic is simple – when you have set a goal, you go after it, now, today, and every day until it is achieved. To do otherwise is to be lazy and weak.

Multiple other successful people have followed the same advice, such as LeBron James NBA star, who despite his talent was known for never taking breaks in the summer. Ted Turner, an American media mogul, and businessman have also spoken highly of perseverance as a necessary element of success. According to Turner, failure isn't an option, and as such, there is no reason to spend time worrying about it, instead of focusing on what you want to do and what you want to achieve is core.

Seneca himself goes on to talk about this by explaining that success was, in fact, accessible to the poorly talented and the low born but was subject to the ability to persevere or to remain unwearied in the face of trials and tribulations. Now, the issue here is that not everyone who is successful or rich is the way they are because they have worked hard and clawed their way to the top through grit and willpower. In fact, some people were born with fortune, while others lucked into it, by lotteries or simply by being at the right place at the right time. Fortune it seems favors fools.

The problem is, luck or fortune cannot be replicated –which is exactly why envy or jealousy happens to be so pointless. Wishing or wanting something isn't going to make it magically drop in your lap, all you are doing is cultivating negativity to feed on later.

The only 'guarantee' that life can offer is that people who persevere, be it through obstacles and difficulties or through pure adversity, will, in the end, be able to master themselves at the very least.

Do you know what it takes to be world-class at something?

10,000 hours of deliberate practice.

Bill Gates before he dropped out of college as a sophomore had 10,000 hours of programming under his belt, fast forward a few years and Microsoft was born. The same goes for the global sensation 'The Beatles', still arguably considered by many to be one of the most iconic bands in history, started out by performing every day of the week in Germany, for over 8 hours each day, and at a point became so in sync with each other that they couldn't help but get better.

As long as you are working hard towards a goal and refusing to give up, you are building in many ways a platform for success. While entrepreneurial ventures also depend largely on what is referred to as the click moment or that moment when everything fits, kind of like seeing a lemonade stand in the middle of a desert. For the most part, business and success in businesses stem from how much effort is consistently being put in to promote success.

So, next time don't focus on the failures or what's not working, instead let your mind accept the failure and move on. In the words of Ryan Holiday,

> *'It's okay to be discouraged. It's not okay to quit. To know you want to quit but to plant your feet and keep inching closer until you take the impenetrable fortress you've decided to lay siege to in your own life – that's persistence.'*

And in our books, persistence and perseverance are just about the same, in terms of the endgame.

Emotional Control

> *'A rational person can find peace by cultivating indifference to things outside their control.' – Naval Ravikant*

And that, of course, brings us all the way back to emotional control.

When it comes to how we act or perceive things, emotional attachment, or emotions; one of the biggest problems is that, more often than we care to admit, we have no idea what we feel, much less how we should deal with it.

The first thing that we need to understand is that despite the fact that Stoics have harped on about emotional control for centuries, what they're saying has an actual footing in modern science as well. As Dr. David Hawkins has proved, there is actual energy that is used when we feel any emotion and these emotions, based on their type, actually promote or destroy cell life. Positive emotions lead to increased energy levels while negative emotions, like rage or scorn, lead to the actual death of cells. Which in turn meant that if we weren't controlling how we felt, how we felt was very literally controlling us, physically.

This is why Marcus Aurelius, in Meditation, goes on to state that we must ensure that the part of our soul that rules us independently aka the brain or the mind, is uninfluenced by the actual actions that happen within your flesh. That is to say, it is able to draw a line between what the body itself and its experiences, such that the experiences do not lead to you attaching some form of judgment, good or bad, to the action that has been visited upon it.

To explain this in the most basic way possible, if you get fired from your job today, or if you fail a job interview – how would you feel about it? What would you think?

Upset? Sad? Angry?

You would think, that something untoward or unwanted had happened and that you were now at a loss because there are loose ends and you don't know what to do next.

This right here is what needs to change.

Being fired is not a bad thing. Being fired from one job as a co-host is what lead Oprah Winfrey to become the most influential female talk show host of her time. Michael Jordan didn't make the cut for his high school basketball team, and Walt Disney was fired from his day job for 'lack of creativity'. And all of these things are what allowed them to become who they became.

The ability to separate how we feel about action from action is critical when it comes to balancing mental health and productivity. So how did all these successful people do it?

Well, simply put they made a choice.

When something happens to you, your emotions may rise and you may act in a certain manner, but if you want, you can control your emotion by exerting your will – be scared, but stand your ground; be mad, but don't act in rage; be sad, but don't wallow in self-pity. These are all active choices that are made by an individual to apply the Stoic principle of reason over emotion.

It sounds a little complicated, doesn't it?

Why don't we teach you an easy way?

Have you ever heard of the emotional wheel?

Okay let's backtrack for a moment – at any given moment, research has shown that only about 36% of people know how they feel and are capable of pinpointing their actual emotions. So, if you're anxious, that can mean that you are overwhelmed but it can also mean that you are worried. If you are tired, it can mean that you are feeling actually physically tired and you're sleepy or it could be that you are feeling powerless.

Why is this important?

Well frankly, because it's hard to control how you feel if you don't *know* how you feel.

Enter the emotional wheel.

The emotional wheel allows individuals who perhaps don't have a clear understanding of how and why they feel the way they feel, to explore the broad general emotion they are experiencing and slowly narrow it down step by step. You start by evaluating your thoughts against one of the six broader emotional categories and then slowly narrow it down to understand exactly what it is they feel.

Once we've figured out what we feel, we shut down the emotional core of our brain and log into the reasoning chamber. Say for instance one is feeling critical. Being critical means that one is either skeptical or they are suspicious about something – now the question is not how we feel but what we do with how we feel?

So, if you are feeling skeptical, you can either be defiant and reject the feeling and create a cycle of frustration and anger; or you can accept how you feel, inquire into the cause or your mental chain of thoughts and then build towards creating a new perspective.

Now, interestingly although these feelings are being felt, they are not being acted on and are instead being submitted for a logical review. This allows us to decide how we want to react. Much like the Stoic concept of volition, we are the rock in the sea against which emotional waves rise, but which stands fast in its own truth.

How to Deal with Adversity

'The more you seek the uncomfortable the more you will be comfortable' - Conor McGregor

One of the core tenets of Stoicism is the ability to deal with difficulty and face obstacles without allowing the challenge to control you. In fact, if you turn to history, you'll actually find that Stoicism has always had a foothold in adversity, it arises like a phoenix from the ashes of charred souls and minds as a way out of the constant struggle that besieges you.

As Marcus Aurelius puts it, the art of life is more of a wrestler's art than it is a dancer's. Unlike dance where the beauty and lesson of art are to gracefully glide through life, in wrestling you are taught to stand your ground and prepare your body and mind to accept the process and deflect unexpected 'onsets', which is basically the basis of Stoicism.

The ability to accept all the problems and obstacles that life will throw your way, to use them as learning curves, and to then take from these instances a clarity and peace of mind that stems directly from your strong sense of self, is the basic goal of Stoic philosophy. In fact, adversity as such is actually anticipated by many Stoic scholars. Seneca once claimed that 'Constant misfortune brings this one blessing; to whom it always assails, it eventually fortifies.'

This is a concept that has actually been the basis for countless success stories, look at the Paralympic gold medalist Marc Zupan. Zupan's ordinary life took a nosedive when a drunk driving accident left the young man not just hurt, but drastically maimed. Zupan lost all four limbs and become a quadriplegic, and life, as he knew, seemed to be taken away from him. When it comes to adversity, it's hard to imagine a harder obstacle to overcome. And yet he did, not only did Zupan win the gold medal for wheelchair rugby, but he also went on to star in the Oscar-nominated movie *Murderball* and was even invited to the White House for his amazing achievements. Now, ask yourself, how would Zupan have done any of that if the accident hadn't happened.

Does this make the accident desirable? Does it mean it was a blessing in disguise?

Absolutely not. The accident wasn't a good thing, the exact same way in which it wasn't a bad thing.

There are no attributes of good or evil, that endure when you are dealing with an event. An event is just that, a happenstance.

The question lies in how you will either react or respond to the issue.

When the billionaire owner of Facebook Mark Zuckerberg, began to develop and seek investments for his company, he faced a seemingly insurmountable obstacle. He was working with a product that basically had no prior business model and therefore, made no sense to investors. An affluent Harvard student, Zuckerberg, could easily have chosen the path of least resistance and gotten a typical job in software development. Instead, he pursued his passion. When it comes to applying Stoicism in business, you will often find that passion becomes the deciding factor – an interesting thought, because any extreme emotion seems to be outside of the Stoic rulebook. But is it really?

Seneca, one of the most iconic Stoic philosophers, has said repeatedly that the means are the only thing that is real and that it is the means that define the end. Here if the goal was the development of Facebook, what were the means?

The simple answer? Action. Persistent action in the face of constant opposition was the way in which Facebook was achieved. Now, yes, the action may have been triggered by passion, but the action itself is a very Stoic notion.

Adversity, when properly approached, is an amazing

opportunity. It's like an instant system reboot. The way you face and approach these issues is what is going to not only hone our skills, it is also going to make sure we are equipped to face reality.

The CEO of Goldman Sachs' once famously stated that he simply did not understand individuals who gave up in the face of adversity. To him, if one failed, even if they failed miserably, the only thing that made sense was for them to move on and try again because no matter how badly they failed, it wasn't going to be the end of the world and the only way to get past these roadblocks was to work harder.

So, how does that apply to you?

What have you given up on recently? What about not so recently? Why did you do it? What did you learn from it? How can you do it better?

That's a lot of questions, but don't worry, we'll wait. Figure out what your problems were and face them head-on. Remember, direct confrontation is the only way to make a Stoicism count.

Chapter 4: Adjusting to the Outside

I have often wondered how it is that every
man loves himself more than all the rest of
men, but yet sets less value on his own
opinion of himself than on the opinion of
others.' – Marcus Aurelius

As odd as it may seem, given the fact that Stoicism preaches the isolation of thought and action, the ability to adjust to the outside world is an important cornerstone of Stoic philosophy. Why?

Well, what do you think separates Stoicism from cynicism?

The acknowledgment and adjustment we make to fit in with our societies and cultures. Stoicism recognizes that we need to work toward making our surroundings a better place, and any good business *must* do the same.

Extrospection: Understanding Others

"When we are no longer able to change a
situation, we are challenged to change
ourselves." – Viktor E. Frankel

Let's then start with extrospection – first of all, what does 'extrospection' even mean? Is it even a real word?

Well, yes, it is!

Now, we all know what introspection means, right? It means to look within yourself to find an answer. Extrospection is the opposite, here you are expected to look outside your mind to assess and acknowledge the circumstances that surround you and then identify our role in relation to these external factors to better understand our own place and our own reactions.

Think about it like this, every time you deal with someone other than yourself and keep in mind that doesn't just mean every time you speak to someone else, it means every time you hear voice, watch a movie, listen to a song, or even read a book that is not written by you – you are opening yourself up to another person and their thoughts. These thoughts, actions, and even just the presence can influence how a person views what they are doing.

Think about how self-conscious you feel answering test questions when your teacher is standing over your shoulder. This is the definition of extrospection – your surroundings influence you, and you understanding how and why is what extrospection is all about!

So, what are the things you need to understand about your surroundings? Three things - Impact, triggers, and support.

Well, for one, you need to understand how the external environment is impacting you. If for instance, you start working at a place where the people around you are low in spirits, don't have good productivity, and are generally negatively minded – when it comes to your own productivity levels, you'll soon find that you are mirroring your co-workers. You will act as you see the people around you act and this is why measuring impact is so important. The more you understand how your surroundings are causing you to behave, be it positive or negative – the more you know what to expect and the better you can plan.

Measuring impact is a more generalized form of extrospection, there is a lot of stuff that happens around us that causes more direct, more specific reactions, which are called triggers. Whereas impact refers to the general circumstances that influence us by default. Triggers are a reference to the more individually targeted actions such as someone telling you that you look good and that comment causing you to feel a surge of happiness and self–confidence take over, that comment has acted as a trigger and made you feel a certain way.

The third thing that you need to check for when you are extrospecting is the nature of the circumstance, how has this been making you feel? Did you feel happy or sad? Were you encouraged or discouraged? Figuring out if you feel supported and more productive is a great way to evaluate the value levels of the external factors that you are dealing with. Even though Stoicism teaches us to focus on our own actions and reactions, aka introspect, a little bit of extrospection goes a long way in terms of business. It puts you in the customer's shoes and gives you a bird's eye view of what is going on around you and how you can better deal with your surroundings.

Long story short, understanding what is driving your thought process is as important as trying to put a leash on your emotions and emotional outbursts and in fact, is actually more important. Since with the right kind of balance, you can use your extrospection to put yourself in situations where you won't be emotionally triggered at all! Win-win!

Emotional Control: The How-to Manual

"Today I escaped anxiety. Or no, I discarded it, because it was within me, in my own perceptions — not outside." — Marcus Aurelius, Meditations

Now, while we've spoken extensively about what emotional control is, what we haven't quite covered is how we are supposed to implement this emotional control system. This is critical, particularly when dealing with other people because our outward expressions of our emotions are what determine much of our character. That is to say, being extremely upset on the inside and happy on the outside creates a kind of Stoic vortex, where you are physically acting in accordance with the philosophy but not mentally taming your mind.

Similarly, when we deal with other people, it is their external expressions of emotions that lead us to assess and react in a specific way.

So, how do we develop emotional control like the Stoics?

Why don't we give you a cheat sheet?

1. Admit, and Acknowledge

For starters, admit that how you feel is an internalized emotion, thought rather than a reality. By doing this, what you are doing is you pulling out of the blame game you were playing up to this point. You see, most of us have a tendency of assigning blame to objects or people outside of ourselves. But in truth doing so is just your mind's way of making excuses for itself.

Let's use an example. Donald is a serial abuser, for over 5 years, he has been abusing his wife Kelly, when he comes home drunk. Every time Donald does so, the next day when he is sober, he claims that the entire incident was Kelly's fault and tells her that she needs to stop making him mad.

Let's translate, what do you think Donald is really saying?

I didn't do it willingly. I was forced to. It's not my fault.

It's the exact same thing you are saying when you are saying you couldn't meet a deadline because of X, Y, and Z or when you are justifying getting upset with another external reason. Take a minute, breathe – and be honest. Isn't the real reason you failed to do it because you prioritized something else. Similarly, the real reason that your emotions are getting the better of you is that you are allowing them to. By admitting this, not only are you admitting that you need to fix something that you're doing, but you're also taking control and accepting the fact that you are capable of taking responsibility and therefore that you are your own master. We do not feel things out of our control, rather we feel things that we teach and allow ourselves to feel.

2. Find Your Own Compass

Once you've taken responsibility, your next job is to figure out a way to hold yourself accountable. Back in the old days, it was easier for Stoics because they had little Stoic 'clubs' where they could hold each other accountable – but what do you do now? Well, you find your own compass. Find out what you need to do, define what is right, and stick to it. It's not always easy and you won't always be able to do it, but what's important is that even if you do stray, you always come back and try again. Seneca, in Letters from a Stoic, suggested that individuals find models or icons to look up to and that they measure themselves against such. If you are a writer facing rejection, look at J.K. Rowling, tell yourself that this woman failed over fifty times before becoming the world's first billionaire author. Remind yourself that every time she was rejected, she worked harder and harder until she got where she is now and use that respect as motivation to keep your impulsive tendency to give up in check. Emotional control is 90% willpower and 10% strategy, ensuring you keep to your true north is all about you staying true to your path, remember that and more importantly act on it.

3. Work On It

Are you a temperamental person? Do you find it hard to keep your temper in check?

Now that you know that, what steps have you taken to address it?

When your emotions hijack your mind and body – the first thing you need to work on is understanding what is triggering you and then you can focus on working on that trigger. So, is your husband telling you that your dress is a little skimpy the problem, or have you been feeling this way for a while based on things he has said before this? Where are your feelings coming from? Can you do anything to change it?

If it is a conflict between people that is leading to your emotional imbalance try talking things out, understand why they said or did what they did and then allow yourself to understand why you are reacting the way you're reacting. Figure out the problem and work on it, and don't stop working on it until it is perfect. Perfection is key. Steve Jobs was often called heartless, but friends have often denied this claim stating that it wasn't that Jobs was heartless, it was merely that the man was a perfectionist and he couldn't stand when people made mistakes.

Emotional outbursts come from a combination of *internal factors* but they all boil down to one thing – we do what we do because we are thinking along specific lines. It is these thoughts that need to change. If your reactions are stemming from fear of failure, counsel yourself on loss aversion. Recognize that failure is not the end of the road and instead challenge yourself to understand your failure – what happened, why didn't it work? Your failures are opportunities, so use them!

Motivation and Inspiration

'How long are you going to wait before you demand the best for yourself?" – Epictetus

And we are back to motivation, but this time we're not just dealing with what motivates us, we are also dealing with what inspires us. Now mankind, in general, is influenced by a myriad of things, starting from the factors we discussed during our bout with extrospection, to other things such as perception and directed inferences but what motivates us and more importantly what teaches us to deal with the world around us?

Well, according to Stoics, motivation is nothing but an impulse and is one of the main areas that Epictetus repeatedly recommends that we train, in order to improve our productivity and more importantly to follow through with our Stoic duty, which is to act deliberately not mindlessly for good reasons.

Sounds pretty complicated, huh?

Let's look at this factor from the point of view of Jack Ma, the Founder, and CEO of Alibaba and AliExpress. Jack Ma has gone around for years explaining that he doesn't run a company, he runs an ecosystem and this was because Jack was a firm believer that he *had* to.

Why? Why did he have to? What was his motivation? Patriotism. Jack Ma firmly believed that if he didn't do what he did with his company, in terms of e-commerce, the Chinese economy would have collapsed and as such, he felt compelled to start AliPay, which was a part of the then unsteady financing sector. Ma did this in spite of people repeatedly warning him that he could end up facing jail time if things went south, and regardless, Ma kept moving forward. Ma's logic was simple, it needed to be done, and it was a virtuous act – who does that remind you of?

So, for starters, we are going to work on developing Stoic motivation, like Ma, and in order to do that, we need to train our perception to avoid negative or positive concepts and instead focus on the notion of natural good.

How do we do that?

Well, let's go old school and use a little checklist again – ready?

1. Train Perception to Avoid Good and Bad

> *"We are more often frightened than hurt, and*
> *we suffer more from imagination than from*
> *reality.' – Seneca*

What Seneca is actually trying to say here, is that we have a tendency to feel what we think we're going to feel and kind of build that up in our head. A modern-day psycho-therapist is known for actually using Seneca's letters as an exercise for his students and a particular incident with one of his patients is actually the most amazing way to really establish the power of perceptive thought.

When Dubois was explaining to one of his patients how Stoic philosophy could help them with their ability to cope with the illness they were dealing with, the patient cut him off and told him that he understood and even offered to explain it to him. Intrigued Dubois sat back and listened, as his patient took out a piece of paper and drew a massive black spot on it and then began to explain himself. The young man pointing to the black spot claimed that the spot was the illness that he was suffering from. He then proceeded to draw a line along the edge of the first circle and said, this is what happens when he focuses on this spot, the spot becomes larger Then if he continues to affirm and obsesses over it, the pain becomes greater still as does the circle.

His point was simple, if you leave pain alone, you don't exacerbate it −in fact, it remains what it is, no more no less. And on the other hand, if you put it in focus, your pain becomes central and everything else begins to rotate around it. The solution here is simple, don't focus on attributes given to actions − actions are stand-alone facts, it is no good to them and there is no evil. Your perception is what adds emotional value to these things and as such, this is what must be controlled.

2. Reflect on Your Own Attention

> *"A key point to bear in mind: The value of attentiveness varies in proportion to its object. You're better off not giving the small things more time than they deserve." —*
> Marcus Aurelius, Meditations

You know how your parents have told you numerous times not to engage bullies and just to ignore them?

Well, negative emotions are mental bullies – so when you allow yourself to wallow in them, be it in rage, in pity, or even in sorrow, what you are doing is you are adding value to something that deserves none. Think about the sheer amount of crimes that are committed due to the fact that the perpetrators want attention – it's the grown-up equivalent to the boy in class with a crush on you pulling your pigtails. Now imagine, if instead of focusing on the perps, the media coverage focused solely on the victims – what has gained value, the bad or the good?

You need to train your mind, the way you wish the global media had been trained. Reflect on the things you are paying the most attention to; is it gossip, or is it an idea that could help change lives? Remember, the attention you give determines the value you are assigning it. Spend your time wisely, it is precious and deserves to be respected.

3. Don't procrastinate

Now it may seem hard, but if you are to work on your self-motivation, you are going to have to start by not being a procrastinator.

Marcus Aurelius discusses this issue in-depth and even provides in his personal journal an extremely inspiring conversation he had with himself, that helped him to find purpose and to use that purpose to expel lethargy and laziness from his own subconscious.

For individuals who suffer from procrastination most of all, in terms of how much they can control their minds, the excerpt is a powerful piece of Stoic purpose that is a great way to start your day, to help train yourself to at least aspire to be better. The Emperor writes -

> *"At dawn, when you have trouble getting out of bed, tell yourself: 'I have to go to work—as a human being. What do I have to complain of, if I'm going to do what I was born for— the things I was brought into the world to do? Or is this what I was created for? To huddle under the blankets and stay warm?*
>
> *—But it's nicer here...*
>
> *So, you were born to feel 'nice'? Instead of*

doing things and experiencing them? Don't
you see the plants, the birds, the ants and
spiders and bees going about their individual
tasks, putting the world in order, as best they
can? And you're not willing to do your job as
a human being? Why aren't you running to
do what your nature demands?

—But we have to sleep sometime...

Agreed. But nature set a limit on that—as it
did on eating and drinking. And you're over
the limit. You've had more than enough of
that. But not of working. There you're still
below your quota. You don't love yourself
enough. Or you'd love your nature too, and
what it demands of you. People who love
what they do wear themselves down doing it,
they even forget to wash or eat. Do you have
less respect for your own nature than the
engraver does for engraving, the dancer for
dance, the miser for money or the social
climber for status? When they're really
possessed by what they do, they'd rather stop
eating and sleeping than give up practicing
their arts."

How to Deal with Disappointment

*"It is in times of security that the spirit should
be preparing itself for difficult times; while
fortune is bestowing favors on it is then is the
time for it to be strengthened against her
rebuffs."*
- Seneca

Stoicism is about more than just motivation and staying away from negative emotions though, it also helps teach you how to deal with the influx of emotions that you face on a day to day basis. In fact, one of the most iconic Stoic practices is the concept of 'negative schooling' – the idea being that you can actually train your brain to be so well prepared for the worst-case scenario, that you will no longer fear it. One of Seneca's personal ideas was to practice your fears. He recommended that for a set number of days each month one should practice what they feared most, such as poverty or starvation. The idea being that by living through these difficulties in a controlled manner you would be prepared to face it, and therefore wouldn't fear. His theory was basically the same as the philosophical version of guerilla training – by preparing for the worst, you overcame the worst.

So, the next time you feel like you are being controlled by fear, allow yourself to experience it. If your fear is a failure, accept failure and allow yourself to fail; failure is never permanent, all you have to do is get back up again. Teach your employees to do the same. Remember the bigger the failure the bigger the effort, which means you are not just overcoming your fear, you are overcoming your inability to get past it!

Rage

'Anybody can become angry – that is easy,
but to be angry with the right person and to
the right degree and at the right time and for
the right purpose, and in the right way – that
is not within everybody's power and is not
easy.' - Aristotle

And finally, you have rage – considered by most Stoic philosophers as the most damaging and worthless emotion in the book. One of the best examples of the damage rage can cause was when Alexander the Great, once engaged in a drunken rage-filled brawl with his best friend Cletius. Unfortunately, Alexander in a fit of rage ended up murdering Cletius and it was only after the act that he realized what he had done.

But by then it was too late. This story is almost the same as any rage-induced outburst ever – think about how many times you did or said something in a fit of rage and then later realized you couldn't take it back. Once you put something out in the universe it is there forever. So when you speak, when you act, and even when you are merely thinking to yourself; if you aren't careful and if you aren't free from 'passion' you risk becoming Alexander, perhaps you won't have lost a life but a relationship, or an opportunity – but you will lose.

Your willpower to focus your thoughts must be unbendable. Every event that you face and every trigger you meet must be an opponent in a judo match, where your job is to sidestep and deftly use the aggression of your attacker against themselves and it is thus that you take back control. Pretty powerful, isn't it?

Chapter 5: Stoicism in the Business World

*'Don't dismiss people, don't be a dick, and
don't rush. Play the long game.'*
Tim Ferris

Now, we've gone through a lot of logic and philosophy, but what we haven't had a chance to do is figure out how any of that affects the whole business end of the deal. Sure, we've seen leaders like Obama, Warren Buffett and the founder of Ikea embody numerous Stoic principles in their own lives and we've seen it work for them, but how do we replicate that?

How do we get Stoicism to work for us and our companies?

Well, for starters, looking at the basics of Stoicism helps to focus on the rational side of issues. The philosophy helps blend the clarity of perspective with pure logic, and that helps entrepreneurs stay grounded and self-aware. The awareness, in turn, causes them to develop clear goals and follow them through with the discipline that is preached through it. Simply put Stoicism acts like a personal anti-virus in our mind's personal operating system, every time a virus, be it social or physical, attacks us; Stoicism is there to protect, deflect, and to clean up the mess left behind.

So, why don't we go through a few common issues that business owners face and address them with Stoic principles?

Sound good?

Without further ado then – here we go!

What to do when Employees Underperform

So, you've been working your way from the ground up and now currently find yourself in charge of an actual team. This in itself would be awesome but unfortunately, the team happens to have one tiny little problem. One certain member of the team is seriously underperforming, to the extent where it has caught the eye of higher management, and now you've been told to take a look into the issue and fix the problem – what do you do and more importantly where do you start?

Why don't we give a checklist?

Here you go!

1. Practice Active Listening:

> *'I begin to speak only when I'm certain what*
> *I'll say isn't better left unsaid."*
> *– Cato the Younger*

Even though it may feel counter-intuitive, the first thing you need to 'do' is absolutely nothing. There is always more than one side to a story and if you don't have all the facts right, not only do you risk blaming someone who could be reacting to a negative stimulator in the group, like a bad team leader perhaps. But you could also, worst-case scenario, be putting yourself in some real legal trouble. Wrongful termination is a big deal and you don't want that on your hands or reputation.

Instead, go in with the intent to listen. This keeps you away from the 'bad boss tag' which is important because remember, you have hundreds of other employees who are watching what's happening. f they see you go in fully charged firing first and asking questions later, they are going to decide that this is what you would do to them too. No one wants to work in a work environment that is negative. Not only does it scare them, but it makes them feel unsafe. This is why in specific professions there are actually built-in safety nets, for instance firing a doctor for medical negligence is actually pretty hard – this is because the law believes that if doctors go into operations scared that they are going to make a mistake and then get fired, they are less likely to go into surgeries and even less likely to go an extra mile to save lives.

Instead, go in with the intention of observing and listening. This not only gives you the information you need, but it also gives it to you from various perspectives, so you can understand the impact as well as your employee's needs.

2. Ask Yourself Questions

'Do not explain your philosophy, embody it.'
– Epictetus

So, you've done your active listening, is it time for you to start talking?

Well, not quite.

Now that you know how and why they are underperforming, you need to take a long hard look at yourself, and at the team – and ask yourself how have you failed them?

While ideally, employees are expected to meet all your set expectations, one thing that is often forgotten, is to check to see if those employees knew what those expectations were. Were they explicitly told and made aware of repercussions?

Even if they were, did you train them accordingly? Be honest, did you ensure that your trainees were equipped to deal with or meet your expectations? Did they even understand them?

If you are faltering when it comes to answering any of these issues, the root issue here is not the lack of performance, but the lack of knowledge and that is what needs to be fortified first. As a Stoic, you cannot assign blame to a person without introspection. Remember, actions are actions, they are not good or bad. Once you take away that element of judgment it is easier to see them for what they are, the result of a sum of other things. Try to understand what this underperformance is a result of and identify which of your own personal actions influenced it.

3. Give Feedback

> 'Use only the appropriate actions of pursuit
> and avoidance, and even these lightly, and

with gentleness and reservation.'

Once you've seen through listening and self-introspection, you are now ready to deal with the issues that relate solely to the employee in question. As the manager, you now have a duty to explain the issues and the expectations in a manner that is honest, but perhaps a little empathetic as well.

Remember, a little compassion goes a long way when it comes to dealing with people, in fact, being kind is a critical component of Stoicism as well. Zeno once said that you should not only be kind and compassionate as you allow people to tell you their problems, but you should also commiserate with them, to the extent that if they are groaning in pain, you should groan too, but only outwardly.

So, keep that in mind as you start talking to your employee, don't be 'blunt' and 'confrontational' – being a bully doesn't make you cool and that is exactly what it would be if you wanted to flex your muscles. Be clear and consistent, but also be nice about it. Tell your employees exactly what is going on, how the company is suffering, how their incomplete task load came to the forefront, and how you and the company have certain expectations of them and what they are.

Furthermore, try not to have the conversation alone – you don't want to be cornering them. Bring in their immediate superior or their line manager and an HR representative, so that they feel the situation is balanced. Remember your job is not to scare them, it is to explain to them what you need and how you need it done by them.

4. Document Everything

*'Don't demand that things happen as you
wish, but wish that they happen as they do
happen, and you will go on well.'*

The next step goes beyond just the boardroom discussion you're about to have. Let's start with the discussion you are having with the employee in question. Keep in mind that documentation or writing things down during the meeting is important because it creates a clear sense of consciousness – not only will your employee clearly hear what you are saying, they'll be able to visualize it and clarify anything they are unclear on.

But documentation is more than a meeting technique, in fact, it is critical for post-intervention follow-ups. So, if you are having problems with the employee, even if you are speaking to them face-to-face, make sure there is documented proof of this; send an email, or a memo containing all the major points and ensure that this is sent to and received by the employee in question.

Basically, think like a lawyer. Ensure that you have proof every step of the way. This doesn't make you strict, this makes you smart. By being thoroughly documented, you are sending a message that says, you are going to be holding them accountable and you are also prepared to do what is necessary to do that. Ideally, you will never need the documents and the scare tactic will be enough, but in case it isn't you at least have what you need to deal with the employee in accordance with company directives.

5. Find Positive Ways to Help instead of Berate

> *'When we are no longer able to change a situation, we are challenged to change ourselves.' — Viktor Frankl*

As you proceed as a leader, it is important to understand that you are dealing with people from a point of power and they are already intimidated by you. A good leader knows that fear is the worst of motivators, instead try using positive reinforcement techniques, like reminding them of how good they used to be or talking to them about the potential they have and use that to show them that they can if they want chose to be better.

It is also important to show them how good performances can and will benefit them. Remember, even though Stoic principles are important, it is also important to learn to adapt them to fit in with the context. Give them a broad goal that helps and benefits the world, but also give them small goals to help motivate them on small scale levels, such as promotions or pay raises.

6. Stick to What You Say

'Other people's mistakes? Leave them to their
makers.' – Marcus Aurelius

In many ways, being a boss is a lot like being a parent and you need to play bad cop sometimes. Even though docking someone's pay because they are late, may seem petty to you, it can be a necessary measure – remember you can't be giving one employee leeway to come in late every day, while other people have to come in on time – that is discrimination and it will lead to massive tension in the group.

Start laying out and enforcing clear consequences – don't just go up and say, you need to come in on time or there will be problems. Call a meeting and clarify that now for every 3 days an employee is late to work, without a valid medical cause or emergency as approved by their line manager, they will be written up and or fired!

Do the same for larger issues as well, if you need a specific task to come in by a specific date, go and talk to the employee in question and explain to them, kindly that you don't want to do this, but if they don't meet the deadline the will be facing a fine, or they won't be eligible for a promotion or whatever else you need to do to keep them in line.

It's great to have compassion for your employees and while that may make you reluctant to actually take proactive steps, you have to remember that other people's mistakes are theirs and they need to face them You can't intervene everywhere and more importantly, you shouldn't.

7. Avoid Trigger Based Self-talk

'The universe is change; our life is what our thoughts make it.'
– Marcus Aurelius

Remember how we talked about rage earlier and how it was considered to be a roadblock, and clearly against Stoic principles – another thing that is clearly against Stoic principles is dosing yourself with negativity. Remember no actions have attributes, which means nothing is good or bad, things simply are.

As such when you are dealing with your problem employee, if you keep dosing yourself with negative back talk – by saying stuff like 'He's so dumb', 'He's doing this on purpose', you are in effect creating a mental context for the actions – you are in a word 'villainizing' your employee, which will make it hard for you later to see their actions from a neutral point of view. So, if you are looking at a missed deadline and thinking 'She's such a lazy person', you are preparing yourself to see only the worst in that particular employee. At the same time, you don't want to be overly optimistic, that's problematic as well.

As a manager, you'll find that you're facing a bit of Goldilocks paradox – you can't be too negative or too positive and need to find a productive mid-way. But it's a bit of a conundrum, how do you do that?

Try adopting a neutral stance – be unbiased. Don't change, 'She's so lazy' to 'She's the most hardworking person I know', change it to 'I don't know enough about her work ethic, but based on this missed deadline I feel she needs to work harder.'. This allows you to acknowledge your own perception so that you don't get carried away with your thoughts and stay accountable for them. Remember, when you deal with one employee you are actually dealing with a whole team. If you are being too positive and giving them too much leeway you risk demoralizing other employees. While if you are too negative, you risk upsetting and scaring the other employees. You have to find your sweet spot.

Once you do, a great way to reinforce this is to engage your employees by opening them up to their individual performance targets. Explain the problems you are dealing with and without getting excited or upset, talk about how they can and need to improve. Keep in mind that it's always better to do this by using 'we' statements since drawing yourself into the mix helps prevent your employee from running scared. Remember this isn't cynicism you're dealing with its Stoicism. The objective is to get the message across in the most compassionate way possible, not just vent your anger and dissatisfaction.

8. Do What You Have to Do

'First, say to yourself what you would be;
then do what you have to do.'

– Epictetus

And finally, let's come down to the dirty groundwork. Sometimes, leaders also need to know when to cut their losses. If you have put ample support and effort into maintaining and cultivating an employee to the highest standard and your employee unable or unwilling to give you a return on those investments, you need to know when to give up hope and do what you have to.

Firing someone can being an unpleasant experience and, as such, is something that many managers and leaders tend to put off. But think of your employees as an extension of yourself. If you contract gangrene, as badly as you may want to keep your hands or legs, it is critical that in the interest of saving yourself, or in this case the rest of your team, you are courageous enough to step up and make the decisions that are necessary. Remember there is a statute of limitations on everything, even second-chances.

The Nuances of Negotiations and Sales

"What's left to be prized? This, I think--to
limit our action or inaction to only what's in

keeping with the needs of our own preparation... by having some self-respect for your own mind and prizing it, you will please yourself and be in better harmony with your fellow human beings, and more in tune with the gods--praising everything they have set in order and allotted you."

--- Marcus Aurelius

Because the principles of Stoicism: perception, action, and persistence mirror good business ideals with such fervor it is in fact very beneficial to look at business issues from the eyes of a Stoic philosopher.

Stoicism, at its core, aspires to logic and rationality while acknowledging the presence of normal human emotions such as anger, grief, or happiness. Because it sets *logos* as a goal, it allows businesses and owners to do the same. When in business you seek the bigger picture, it is important that you look at things logically and rationally, not with fear or anxiety or even with optimism. By infusing our business acumen with a little bit of Stoic philosophy we are opening ourselves up to a rational world where we act like the wisest of men, with reason instead of emotion and as such work more consciously and consistently to a greater good.

Sounds pretty fancy, doesn't it?

Why don't we take a look at how we can do that?

1. Business Partners

*"There's nothing worse than a wolf
befriending sheep. Avoid false friendship at
all costs. If you are good, straightforward,
and well-meaning it should show in your
eyes and not escape notice."*

—Marcus Aurelius

One of the most important things you'll find yourself dealing with when it comes to your business is, of course, the people you choose to go into business with. So, who should you go into business with?

Well, that's a rather subjective question, however, why don't you try asking what type of people you should go into a partnership with? The answer to that is fairly simple, people who share the same philosophy and vision. Always remember that your business partners are like your spouse but in a corporate sense.

While dealing with business partners can be a bit tricky, there are actually three cardinal rules to picking a good business partner and they are all based on Stoic principles – why don't you see if they make sense to you and can help you figure who would be a better fit for you and your company?

a. Pick Ambition not Greed

There is a saying that pigs get fat, while hogs get slaughtered – the same goes for people when you are dealing with business partners you want to pick someone who is ambitious and will always help move the company forward. Picking someone who is greedy can actually harm the company in the long run, not only do you not want that but you'll have a hard time making any negotiations with someone who only sees the money, which will make taking risks harder. While that may sound like a good thing, it's actually a really bad thing because it will almost definitely cause your company to stagnate. So, the next time you are picking business partners, ask questions that help you get a feel of what their main goal is, what are they in it for – the money or the product.

b. **Be Teammates not opponents**

The next thing you need to do is ensure that the person you are partnering up with is someone who you can go into an actual team relationship with. Once you become a partner you need to be able to play together, so someone with drastically different morals or ideas will be hard to accommodate when it comes to making delicate company decisions.

c. **See the Big Picture**

Next up is your ability to see the big picture. Is this someone you can see yourself running the company within 10 or 20 years? Don't just pick someone who would fit in the short-term, you can hire consultants for that. In a partnership, this needs to be someone who would do for you as they would for themselves and you need to do the same – try to go for an even 50-50 split, so that the partnership isn't just benefiting one side and has the emotional investment from both ends.

2. Clients

"Crimes often return to their teacher."

—Seneca

Negotiating with clients can be tricky, particularly since in order to keep the business up and running it's hard to be willing to lose a client. Playing hardball, therefore, is a particularly sore point, especially in this economy. Regardless, there are a number of things you need to know and a bunch of principles you need to hold true to or else you're going to end up running your business into the ground.

Remember when it comes to negotiating, emotion running loose is an emotion that is going to cost you. Start by making sure you have your priorities in order, what are you willing to negotiate on, and what is an absolute no go for you? Identify them and list them so that you don't get caught up in the moment and do something untoward. Once you've figured out what you're willing to compromise on, also work on how much you are willing to compromise, what is your hard limit and what is your soft limit. If you can't meet at least one of these, you need to walk away. Giving away more now is not the solution, there will always be other opportunities. Another tip is to never be over-invested. Don't look at any client as your only hope, if they stay they stay but you can't compromise on your business to keep them. This is not only detrimental to the company in the long run, but it can also lead to you giving out unreciprocated concessions that will cost you in the short-term as well.

Do exactly how much you can afford to continue to do, in fact, under-promise and over-deliver. Word of mouth promotion is much better than any other form of PR.

3. Employees

"For I believe a good king is from the outset and by necessity a philosopher, and the philosopher is from the outset a kingly person."

—*Musonius Rufus*

And finally, you are back to employees. this time though, you aren't dealing with the problem child, you're dealing with the star kid who you want to keep on the team. Now, just as it's important to know how to deal with underperforming staff, it's even more important to know how to deal with good staff. After all, staff retention is a huge part of boosting company productivity.

So, what to do you do?

Start by figuring out what they want, remember, preferences need to be assessed carefully so that you not only know what your employees are thinking but also what they want and why.

The best way to do this is to have a clear discussion that promotes integrative negotiation so that you can both walk away feeling like you've won something. Also try to keep your employees happy, remember a happy employee is an efficient employee. If you need to invest in training or perhaps talk about job facilities that can help promote happiness, that is exactly where you need to start.

Stress and Anxiety

"When I see an anxious person, I ask myself, what do they want? For if a person wasn't wanting something outside of their own control, why would they be stricken by anxiety?"

—Epictetus

Management and strategies aside though, Stoic philosophy's biggest role in terms of business and in particular modern-day entrepreneurial businesses is its ability to not only mitigate but actually deal with and address the immense stress and anxiety that comes along with creating something with no safety net.

Stoicism helps people not only seek and find value, but it also teaches them to acknowledge and adapt to the surroundings they are in, which helps us constantly move forward. At the same time, it helps us stay grounded in thought and actions so that we can ensure we are doing things for all the right reasons and aren't running after things that are either unfeasible or unworthy.

Striking Balance – Find Personal Value

> *"Don't be bounced around, but submit every impulse to the claims of justice, and protect your clear conviction in every appearance."*

> —*Marcus Aurelius*

When you are dealing with a new venture, it is natural that not everyone will see what you see, and not everyone will believe in your project as you do. As a person and as a business leader, you need to be able to accept and understand every other opinion you come across without reacting like a four-year-old throwing a temper tantrum. At the same time, you also need to not waver with every negative opinion so much so that you can't hold on to your own convictions.

Stand strong and steady. Jeff Bezos of Amazon, once noted that a good businessman knew when to stand firm in their convictions and at the same time knew how and when to be flexible on the little things such as details. He used the example of his own company, stating that while the company's overarching vision never changed, the intricate details did, vastly. This was particularly due to the fact that for many of the smaller things, the way he had thought things would work, just didn't pan out and that they had to change all of that keeping the big picture in mind. The bottom line is that you need to listen to opinions as they will help you grow and stabilize, but they are a dime a dozen, so you don't necessarily have to follow them.

Everything Ends

> *"Many are harmed by fear itself, and many may have come to their fate while dreading fate."*
>
> —Seneca

What else do you need to keep in mind?

That nothing is constant and nothing is forever.

Running a business can be a time-consuming venture. Not only that, but it can also be overwhelming. How many other people do you know who have let their job or their business take over their whole life, while health and relationships got shot to hell?

Probably more than you care to mention. But the truth is that life ends, everything does frankly. Your life, your business, your legacy, all of it will come to an end at some point. So why are you giving it all up?

What is the purpose?

Stoics believe that the purpose of all things is happiness – and as such, happiness is both the end goal and the purpose of the journey. Keep that in mind the next time you look at your venture. Don't moan about not becoming a multi-billion-dollar outfit, be thankful and happy that you have encountered great profits in your first year and that you are still sustaining and growing. You can't always figure out where you are going to be in a year, but you can always be thankful for where you are today.

Accept What You Cannot Control

"I don't agree with those who plunge headlong into the middle of the flood and who, accepting a turbulent life, struggle daily in great spirit with difficult circumstances. The wise person will endure that, but won't choose it—choosing to be at peace, rather than at war."

—Seneca

Another important lesson is acceptance. We have an unfortunate tendency to stress out and get all anxious about a million and one things that we usually don't have a whole lot of control over. Think about product-market viability, let's say you have a product that is perfect for the market and consumer base – but just days before the launch, your investor pulls out or a corporate spy takes your idea and sells it to another company. All that effort all that energy and it's all gone to waste.

Sucks doesn't it – makes you want to go crawl into a hole in the wall and stay there forever.

You know what Stoicism says though? – Go with the flow.

If it happens, it happens. It's not something to be over the moon about. It is an advantage and treats it like one, but don't treat it like it's the only opportunity you'll ever have because that makes it harder to let go. It means that on the off chance that things don't work out and you don't win that tender or secure that investor, it sucks, but it's not the end of the world. Life lesson? Dial down the drama in your head and you'll find the drama in your life will take a nosedive as well.

Be Compassion Driven

"The soul becomes dyed with the color of its thoughts.'

–Seneca

You become who you emulate. And because this is true, it is super important to ensure that the business you run or the focus you hold is not to be the most successful person in the world, no matter what – that would make you Donald Trump, detestable and unpalatable by society at large. Instead, try the opposite. Be kind and compassionate wherever there is an opportunity to be so – be it in the way you run your company, your behavior towards your company, your attitude towards your consumer base, or even your attitude towards nature. Wherever it is and whatever it is you do – you need to start with compassion, so that you can end there as well.

Obstacles are Opportunities

"Once you start learning from your problems, you stop wishing for a life without problems."

– Mokokoma Mokhonoana

The last but perhaps most important lesson that you will find in Stoic business philosophy is the Stoic view on obstacles. When it comes to building a company, you will find that you are faced with numerous challenges on a daily basis. It could be something as simple as an unhappy customer or a bad employee, it could even be a technical problem like an issue with the product line.

But if there is one certainty, it is that there will be *some* sort of a problem. At the moment, that problem may seem like a curse and you'll be exasperated or even discouraged, you'll feel helpless and you won't see the point of all your hard work. But that is the short run.

In the long run, you will find that every single one of these problems was a blessing – they taught you an important lesson about customer service, or product management, or even team building. Whatever it is, whatever you learned, you learned thanks to that obstacle. So the next time you see a problem coming your way, welcome it with open arms. Your product is about to get that much better and your company that much more efficient, which is perhaps the very definition of a blessing in disguise.

Chapter 6: Stoicism in the Real World

"Your potential, the absolute best you're capable of — that's the metric to measure yourself against. Your standards are. Winning is not enough. People can get lucky and win. People can be assholes and win. Anyone can win. But not everyone is the best possible version of themselves."

— Ryan Holiday

And finally, let's come down to the real world. Stoicism has been giving us a lot of information about what we can do in terms of our mental and philosophical growth, particularly in terms of who we want to be and how to get there as a business leader and as an individual.

But how do we do really get this started?

Knowing *why* we should do it and that we *should* do it is different than creating an actual roadmap.

So, why don't we start there – with an actual road-map a 90-day plan to get you to be your Stoic best!

What do you think? Sound exciting?

Why don't you grab yourself a pen and a piece of paper and we'll get right to it!

Go on, we'll wait!

Back?

So, there are just two main things you are going to need to focus on in order to get your Stoic mojo going. The first is to plan like Stoic master and the second is to give your planning a little human spin by putting it into a structure that you are used to. We'll start by showing you how to use Stoic planning, Stoic analytics, and developmental Stoicism specifically to help you create a clear outline for your days. Then we'll take all that and dump it into a Stoic style journal so that you have your Stoic road map for the next three months all planned out – how does that sound?

Well, then without further ado!

We are *off*!

Stoic Planning and Stratagems

The best way to deal with Stoicism and its practice is by thinking of Stoicism as a habit instead of a task – if you tell yourself it is a task, you will find it hard to deal with and more importantly you will find it hard to use as a tool. Instead, recognize that Stoic principles are like lanterns guiding a midnight walker – all you have to do is allow them to light the way.

Three key Stoic actions are to reflect, to evaluate, and to consciously attempt to implement logos in the world around you. By shedding the burden of emotional baggage you are preparing your mind and your soul for the endless possibilities that surround it.

Keep this in mind.

You are powerful.

You are capable.

And most importantly you are willing.

Now, why don't we take all that will and hard work and direct it to the development and maintenance of a Stoic lifestyle through the Stoic form of journaling!

The Importance of Journaling and Maintaining a Schedule

"Could bitching and moaning on paper for
five minutes each morning change your life?
As crazy as it might seem, I believe the
answer is yes."

– Tim Ferriss

Journaling is central to Stoic philosophy and has been a part of the lives of all three major Stoics, so much so, that Marcus Aurelius's most famous piece of literary work, *Meditations*, actually comes from his personal journal and was never really meant to be published. All three philosophers, Seneca the Younger, Marcus Aurelius, and Epictetus all had their own ways of journaling. Marcus Aurelius, for instance, preferred to journal in the morning and would use the act as a form of self-medication to set the tone for the rest of his day. Seneca the Younger, on the other hand, was a night owl and preferred to journal late at night when his wife had gone to sleep. He took his journaling to be an opportunity to look back on his day. A form of introspections and self-reflection that was also seen in Epictetus, who journaled both during the day and at night, advocated the same, stating "Every day and night keep thoughts like these at handwrite them, read them aloud, talk to yourself and others about them."

But how far does this go in terms of modern-day practitioners?

Journaling 101

'Genuine happiness can only be achieved
when we transform our way of life from the
unthinking pursuit of pleasure to one
committed to enriching our inner lives, when
we focus on 'being more' rather than simply
having more'

– Nassim Nicholas Taleb

Since journaling is a little on the complicated side, if you really want to involve Stoic philosophy into your daily routine, we're going to go ahead and give you a 90-day road map – meaning every day for ninety days, we are about to chalk out a prompt specific journal entry to help you dig deep and find your inner

Stoic.

If you're just listening, you can rewind back to this point and note down the prompt and questions for yourself each day, or alternatively, if you are holding the e-book, you can copy or print out the relevant pages so that you have the perfect format in front of you.

In the first 10 days, we are going to work on understanding ourselves and how we feel and see the world. In the next ten days, we'll focus on planning the days in advance. The plans will stay constant each month to help you create a sense of routine and will then be followed by self-reflection. On the final ten days of the month, we'll work on and analyze how our days went and what we learned from them. And then we'll do it all over again for two more months until journaling becomes a part of our daily lives – so, are you ready?

If you want to be productive:

- Go to:

  https://businessleadershipplatform.com/stoic-quotes-business-pdf

  Or use the QR code

- Get the **3-Month-Stoic-Self-Evaluation-Journal** and the **Stoic Quotes**
- print both

Month One

Daily Self-Evaluation

Day One

Date:

Time:

Quote: 'Be happy for this moment, this moment is your life.''- Marcus Aurelius

Questions: What am I grateful for today? What are the things that bring me joy? How have these things impacted my life?

Day Two

Date:

Time:

Quote: 'As long as you live, keep learning how to live.' - Seneca

Questions: What are the things I am doing wrong? What did I do wrong today? How can I avoid doing this tomorrow?

Day Three

Date:

Time:

Quote: 'How much more grievous are the consequences of anger, than the causes of it?' Marcus Aurelius

Questions: When was the last time you dealt with an

uncontrollable fit of anger? What was about? How did it benefit you? How did it harm you?

Day Four

Date:

Time:

Quote: 'Keep company with only the people who uplift you.'- Epictetus

Questions: Who are the people who uplift you? How do you feel around them? Who are the people who don't uplift you? Why do you stay near them?

Day Five

Date:

Time:

Quote: 'Curb your desire – don't set your heart on so many things and you will get what you need.' - Epictetus

Questions: What are the things you desire? What are the things you need? Why do you think there is a difference?

Day Six

Date:

Time:

Quote: 'I do not forget any good deed done to me and I do not carry a grudge for a bad one.' Viktor Fankel

Questions: Why do find it hard to forget wrongs done to you? What was the last good deed that was done for you? How would you compare them?

Day Seven

Date:

Time:

Quote: 'To be wronged is nothing unless you continue to remember it.' - Confucius

Questions: Why do you feel wronged? What was done to you that you feel was unfair? Why do you find it hard to forget?

Day Eight

Date:

Time:

Quote: 'We cannot choose our external circumstance, but we can always choose how we respond to them.' - Epictetus

Questions: What do you choose to perceive differently today? How did you perceive this previously? Is it hard to change your perception?

Day Nine

Date:

Time:

Quote: 'We cannot control the evil tongues of others, but a good life enables us to disregard them.' - Cato

Questions: How do you plan to live a good life? How is this helping you to move past the things that people have said? Why did what they say matter?

Day Ten

Date:

Time:

Quote: 'Life isn't about finding yourself, life is about creating yourself.' – George Bernard Shaw

Questions: Who do you want to be? What are the qualities you want to grow in yourself? Who would you consider your model, and why?

Plan Your Day

Day Eleven

Date:

Time:

Daily Stoic Tasks: Refuse to react in anger, no matter how high the temptation.

Questions: What is the cause of your anger? Why do you feel angry? What did you feel like doing out of anger? What would the consequences of this be?

Day Twelve

Date:

Time:

Daily Stoic Tasks: Refuse to give in to sorrow.

Questions: What is the cause of your sorrow? Why do you feel sad? What leads to you feeling sad? What would be sad accomplish?

Day Thirteen

Date:

Time:

Daily Stoic Tasks: Refuse to feel despair.

Questions: What is the cause of your despair? Why do you feel upset? How did it make you feel? What did you want to do?

Day Fourteen

Date:

Time:

Daily Stoic Tasks: Refuse to feel disgusted.

Questions: What is the cause of your disgust? Why do you think it triggered that particular feeling? Why do you disapprove?

Day Fifteen

Date:

Time:

Daily Stoic Tasks: Refuse to anticipate and draw expectations.

Questions: What do you normally expect? How would you feel without it? Why is it important to you?

Day Sixteen

Date:

Time:

Daily Stoic Tasks: Refuse to be overjoyed.

Questions: What is the cause of your joy? Why is it of such high value? What would it feel like to be let down now?

Day Seventeen

Date:

Time:

Daily Stoic Tasks: Refuse to feel shame.

Questions: Why do you think you should be ashamed? Who has deemed this to be shameful? Does this contradict with the

Stoic principle of virtue?

Day Eighteen

Date:

Time:

Daily Stoic Tasks: Refuse to envy.

Questions: What is the cause of your jealousy? Why do you feel jealous? What did you wish was yours? What would the value of this be?

Day Nineteen

Date:

Time:

Daily Stoic Tasks: Refuse to be helpless.

Questions: Why do you feel helpless? What holds you back? What do you need to be powerful?

Day Twenty

Date:

Time:

Daily Stoic Tasks: Refuse to feel contempt.

Questions: What is the cause of your contempt? Who do you feel contempt for? What did they do to make you feel that they are unworthy of consideration?

Daily Reflections

Day Twenty One

Date:

Time:

Daily Stoic Reflection: Who did you interact with today? How did they make you feel?

Day Twenty-Two

Date:

Time:

Daily Stoic Reflection: What did you do today? How was it difficult?

Day Twenty Three

Date:

Time:

Daily Stoic Reflection: What should you have done today? Why did you not?

Day Twenty Four

Date:

Time:

Daily Stoic Reflection: How was your day? What could have made it better?

Day Twenty-Five

Date:

Time:

Daily Stoic Reflection: When was the best time of your day? What made it special?

Day Twenty-Six

Date:

Time:

Daily Stoic Reflection: Who did you think of today? Why were they on your mind?

Day Twenty-Seven

Date:

Time:

Daily Stoic Reflection: What is the concern you faced today? What do you think you can do about it?

Day Twenty-Eight

Date:

Time:

Daily Stoic Reflection: What is a positive thing you did today? How do you think that will help people?

Day Twenty Nine

Date:

Time:

Daily Stoic Reflection: When is it hard for you to get through the day? What do you have to do to keep going?

Day Thirty

Date:

Time:

Daily Stoic Reflection: What healthy choices did you make today? What could you have done to improve them?

Month Two

Daily Self-Evaluation

Day One

Date:

Time:

Quote: 'Adapt yourself to the life you have been given; truly love the people with whom destiny has surrounded you.'- Marcus Aurelius

Questions: What adaptations do you think you need to make? Why is it hard for you to make them? Who are the people around you? What makes it hard to love them?

Day Two

Date:

Time:

Quote: 'One of the most beautiful qualities of friendship is to understand and to be understood.' - Seneca

Questions: What are the things you are grateful for in your friendships? Who is this friend? How do they make you feel?

Day Three

Date:

Time:

Quote: 'Is a world without pain possible? Then don't ask the impossible.' Marcus Aurelius

Questions: What is making you feel pain? How does this pain feel? Why is it able to hurt you? What does it make you think of?

Day Four

Date:

Time:

Quote: 'The more we value things outside our control, the less control we have.'- Epictetus

Questions: What is outside of your control? Why do you hold it in a position of value? Why does this take away control from you?

Day Five

Date:

Time:

Quote: 'A ship should not ride on a single anchor nor life on a single hope.' - Epictetus

Questions: What is something you hope for? How would you feel if you don't get it? How can you overcome not having it?

Day Six

Date:

Time:

Quote: 'Not to assume it's impossible because you find it hard. But to recognize that if it's humanly possible, you can do it too.'

Questions: Why do you think certain things seem impossible to you? What are they? How do you think you can overcome these problems?

Day Seven

Date:

Time:

Quote: 'If it is not right do not do it, if it is not true do not say it.' – Marcus Aurelius

Questions: What wrong things have you done in life? How does it feel to lie? How often do you lie to yourself? What do you lie about?

Day Eight

Date:

Time:

Quote: 'Hold, unhappy man, be not swept along with your impression! Great is the struggle, divine the task; the prize is a kingdom, freedom, serenity, peace.' - Epictetus

Questions: What do you think Epictetus is talking about here? What impressions do you have? What struggles do you face? What would be your kingdom?

Day Nine

Date:

Time:

Quote: 'It is a rough road that leads to the heights of greatness.' - Seneca

Questions: What difficulties have you faced when trying to succeed? What has been your biggest obstacle? How did you overcome it?

Day Ten

Date:

Time:

Quote: 'Waste no more time arguing what a good man should be. Be one.' – Marcus Aurelius.

Questions: Who do you consider to be a good man? What

defines good for you? How would you aspire to be a good person?

Plan Your Day

Day Eleven

Date:

Time:

Daily Stoic Tasks: Refuse to react in anger, no matter how high the temptation.

Questions: What is the cause of your anger? Why do you feel angry? What did you feel like doing out of anger? What would the consequences of this be?

Day Twelve

Date:

Time:

Daily Stoic Tasks: Refuse to give in to sorrow.

Questions: What is the cause of your sorrow? Why do you feel sad? What leads to you feeling sad? What would be being sad accomplish?

Day Thirteen

Date:

Time:

Daily Stoic Tasks: Refuse to feel despair.

Questions: What is the cause of your despair? Why do you feel upset? How did it make you feel? What did you want to do?

Day Fourteen

Date:

Time:

Daily Stoic Tasks: Refuse to feel disgusted.

Questions: What is the cause of your disgust? Why do you think it triggered that particular feeling? Why do you disapprove?

Day Fifteen

Date:

Time:

Daily Stoic Tasks: Refuse to anticipate and draw expectations.

Questions: What do you normally expect? How would you feel without it? Why is it important to you?

Day Sixteen

Date:

Time:

Daily Stoic Tasks: Refuse to be overjoyed.

Questions: What is the cause of your joy? Why is it of such high value? What would it feel like to be let down now?

Day Seventeen

Date:

Time:

Daily Stoic Tasks: Refuse to feel shame.

Questions: Why do you think you should be ashamed? Who has deemed this to be shameful? Does this contradict with the Stoic principle of virtue?

Day Eighteen

Date:

Time:

Daily Stoic Tasks: Refuse to envy.

Questions: What is the cause of your jealousy? Why do you feel jealous? What did you wish was yours? What would the value of this be?

Day Nineteen

Date:

Time:

Daily Stoic Tasks: Refuse to be helpless.

Questions: Why do you feel helpless? What holds you back? What do you need to be powerful?

Day Twenty

Date:

Time:

Daily Stoic Tasks: Refuse to feel contempt.

Questions: What is the cause of your contempt? Who do you feel contempt for? What did they do to make you feel that they are unworthy of consideration?

Daily Reflections

Day Twenty One

Date:

Time:

Daily Stoic Reflection: What did you do today? What did you want to do in addition? Why did you not do it?

Day Twenty-Two

Date:

Time:

Daily Stoic Reflection: What is the most positive thing that you saw today? How did it affect your perception?

Day Twenty Three

Date:

Time:

Daily Stoic Reflection: What responsibilities did you carry today? How many did you fulfill? What did you miss?

Day Twenty Four

Date:

Time:

Daily Stoic Reflection: What was the most difficult part of your day today? Why was it difficult? How could you have changed this?

Day Twenty-Five

Date:

Time:

Daily Stoic Reflection: When was the worst time of your day? What made it so difficult?

Day Twenty-Six

Date:

Time:

Daily Stoic Reflection: What was your strongest emotion today? Why did you feel it? How do you think your feelings were communicated?

Day Twenty-Seven

Date:

Time:

Daily Stoic Reflection: What is something that disturbed you today? What did you want to do about it? What did you do about it?

Day Twenty-Eight

Date:

Time:

Daily Stoic Reflection: What is a negative thing you did today? How do you think that will harm people? How has it harmed you?

Day Twenty Nine

Date:

Time:

Daily Stoic Reflection: What was the kindness you experienced today? Who was kind to you? What did you do in return?

Day Thirty

Date:

Time:

Daily Stoic Reflection: How calm were you today? On a scale of 1-10, how would you rank your calmness? How did it make you feel?

Month Three

Daily Self-Evaluation

Day One

Date:

Time:

Quote: 'Ask: What is so unbearable about this situation? Why can't you endure it? You will be embarrassed to answer.'- Marcus Aurelius

Questions: What unbearable situation do you feel you are in? Why do you find it to be unbearable? Why are you finding it hard to deal with? Why do you think you would be embarrassed?

Day Two

Date:

Time:

Quote: 'Lives badly who does not know to die well.' - Seneca

Questions: What are the things you do that make you feel that you should live a better life? How can you do that? What do you think about death?

Day Three

Date:

Time:

Quote: 'The first rule is to keep an untroubled spirit, the second is to look things in the face and know them for what they are.' Marcus Aurelius

Questions: What is an untroubled spirit? How do you gain an untroubled spirit? What do you need to look in the face?

Day Four

Date:

Time:

Quote: 'Remain calm in every situation because peace equals power.'- Joyce Meyer

Questions: What is the hardest thing about staying calm? Where do you need to stay calm the most? Why do you think peace is powerful?

Day Five

Date:

Time:

Quote: 'Any person capable of angering you becomes your master; he can anger you only when you permit yourself to be disturbed by him.' - Epictetus

Questions: What is something that angers you? Who causes this anger? Why do you allow this anger to form?

Day Six

Date:

Time:

Quote: 'First learn the meaning of what you say, and then speak.'

Questions: What have you said that you did not understand? What did you say that you wish you had thought of more?

Day Seven

Date:

Time:

Quote: 'You can't calm the storm, so stop trying. What you can do is calm yourself. The storm will pass.' – Timber Hawkeye

Questions: What do you need to do to calm yourself? How have you tried to do so? What was effective? What was not effective?

Day Eight

Date:

Time:

Quote: 'Be strong. Because things will get better. It may be stormy now, but it never rains forever.' – Winston Churchill

Questions: What do you think you should do to stay mentally strong? What is your most difficult moment? Why is it hard to overcome?

Day Nine

Date:

Time:

Quote: 'Learning to ignore things is one of the greatest paths to inner peace.' – Robert J. Sawyer

Questions: What difficulties have you faced when trying to ignore something that bothers you? What has been your biggest hardship? How do you think you can come to terms with it?

Day Ten

Date:

Time:

Quote: 'Never let the future disturb you. You will meet it, if you have to, with the same weapons of reason which today arm you against the present.' – Marcus Aurelius.

Questions: What do you expect of the future? What daunts you? What do you find inspiring?

Plan Your Day

Day Eleven

Date:

Time:

Daily Stoic Tasks: Refuse to react in anger, no matter how high the temptation.

Questions: What is the cause of your anger? Why do you feel angry? What did you feel like doing out of anger? What would the consequences of this be?

Day Twelve

Date:

Time:

Daily Stoic Tasks: Refuse to give in to sorrow.

Questions: What is the cause of your sorrow? Why do you feel sad? What leads to you feeling sad? What would be being sad accomplish?

Day Thirteen

Date:

Time:

Daily Stoic Tasks: Refuse to feel despair.

Questions: What is the cause of your despair? Why do you feel upset? How did it make you feel? What did you want to do?

Day Fourteen

Date:

Time:

Daily Stoic Tasks: Refuse to feel disgusted.

Questions: What is the cause of your disgust? Why do you think it triggered that particular feeling? Why do you disapprove?

Day Fifteen

Date:

Time:

Daily Stoic Tasks: Refuse to anticipate and draw expectations.

Questions: What do you normally expect? How would you feel without it? Why is it important to you?

Day Sixteen

Date:

Time:

Daily Stoic Tasks: Refuse to be overjoyed.

Questions: What is the cause of your joy? Why is it of such high value? What would it feel like to be let down now?

Day Seventeen

Date:

Time:

Daily Stoic Tasks: Refuse to feel shame.

Questions: Why do you think you should be ashamed? Who has deemed this to be shameful? Does this contradict with the Stoic principle of virtue?

Day Eighteen

Date:

Time:

Daily Stoic Tasks: Refuse to envy.

Questions: What is the cause of your jealousy? Why do you feel jealous? What did you wish was yours? What would the value of this be?

Day Nineteen

Date:

Time:

Daily Stoic Tasks: Refuse to be helpless.

Questions: Why do you feel helpless? What holds you back? What do you need to be powerful?

Day Twenty

Date:

Time:

Daily Stoic Tasks: Refuse to feel contempt.

Questions: What is the cause of your contempt? Who do you feel contempt for? What did they do to make you feel that they are unworthy of consideration?

Daily Reflections

Day Twenty One

Date:

Time:

Daily Stoic Reflection: What was your greatest temptation today? What did you want to do? Why did you not do it?

Day Twenty-Two

Date:

Time:

Daily Stoic Reflection: What is something you find kind and loving, that you experience daily? How does it affect your mood?

Day Twenty Three

Date:

Time:

Daily Stoic Reflection: What responsibilities did you fail to carry out today? How many? Why did you fail? How are you going to make this up?

Day Twenty Four

Date:

Time:

Daily Stoic Reflection: What was the biggest blessing you had today? When did it happen? How thankful do you feel?

Day Twenty-Five

Date:

Time:

Daily Stoic Reflection: When was the worst time of your day? What made it so difficult?

Day Twenty-Six

Date:

Time:

Daily Stoic Reflection: What was your weakest emotion today? Why do you think it was weak? How do you feel about it?

Day Twenty-Seven

Date:

Time:

Daily Stoic Reflection: What is something that inspired you today? How do you wish to emulate it? How are you going to see through this thought?

Day Twenty-Eight

Date:

Time:

Daily Stoic Reflection: What is a positive thing that you plan to do tomorrow? How is it positive? Who does it benefit?

Day Twenty Nine

Date:

Time:

Daily Stoic Reflection: How would you define inner peace? What do you think you can do that would help you create inner peace for your own self?

Day Thirty

Date:

Time:

Daily Stoic Reflection: How meaningful did your life feel

today? Why do you think about this? How can you add more meaning?

And just like that, you are done with 90 whole days of Stoic living. Give yourself a pat on the back! This is gladiator level persistence and you deserve every bit of the mental celebration you have going right now. Just remember, you can't just do ninety days and quit, that's like relapsing after going 90 days sober.

Big no-no.

Instead, why don't you take a quick minute and flip back through the 90 days you have done to see how much your answers have changed from day one to your final Day 30?

Not only will that help you better understand how far you've come, but it'll also help you work on where you want to go from here. Where is your Stoic lifestyle going to take you now? Who are you going to be? How are you going to use these new habits to improve the productivity levels of your life and career?

And most importantly, who are you going to be?

You'll be answering all this, so do you think you're ready?

Conclusion

'I have often wondered how it is that every man loves himself more than all the rest of men, but yet sets less value on his own opinion of himself than on the opinion of others.' – Marcus Aurelius

Whew! That was quite the ride wasn't it – it's been a loooong journey, hasn't it?

Well, to begin though, let us take a moment to thank you for buying "Stoicism for Business - *Ancient stoic wisdom and practical advice for building mental toughness, productivity habits and success in modern management*"- we sincerely hope that the book has been able to help you effectively and systematically develop your ability to deal with emotions and life in general, in a more efficient and productive manner just as our Stoic ancestors did.

Now although we have already made a point to cover all of the relevant Stoic philosophies that can and do impact your life, we've also gone on to illustrate how noted world leaders and successful innovators have been using Stoic philosophy as a tool to build their success! There is a reason we did that! The fact that you picked this book up tells us that even if you haven't already started to establish your own company and have things running, you've been thinking about a business venture for some time now and haven't quite been sure how to prepare. Well, your wait is officially over!

Now with the right kind of effort and support, you could be one of the future Stoic success stories and join the ranks of Mark Zuckerberg and Warren Buffet (imagine that!) – but that's only if you make sure you are actually following the Stoic regimen, of course. Stoic living is almost like a fitness plan, it's a lifestyle choice that you are going to have to stick to if you really want to see results. Not only does Stoic living teach us restraint and perspective, but it also teaches us persistence and perseverance both of which are necessary if you are looking to build your empire, and if you're thinking of starting small, this is even more important!

But that's not it, in the words of Marcus Aurelius, 'In your actions don't procrastinate. In your conversations, don't confuse. In your thoughts, don't wander. In your soul, don't be passive or aggressive. In your life, don't be all about business'. The Stoic journey you just finished has an overarching purpose that goes beyond preparing you for a successful career. It's also meant to help you find true happiness and content. Your well-being, your ability to process, your mental peace; all of these are factors that we are deeply invested in – this isn't just your journey, it's *our* journey and we need for you to be happy and content at the end of it.

And we've really gone in-depth to show you how – starting from grassroots level Stoic philosophy, the book also deals with practical application techniques and plans that can and will help you cultivate a Stoic mind if you so choose. But it doesn't end just yet!

If you enjoyed reading this, a few of the other books that you definitely would love to read are Meditations by Marcus Aurelius, The Daily Stoic by Ryan Holiday, Epistulae Morales ad Lucilium by Seneca, A Guide to the Good Life: The Ancient Art of Stoic Joy by William B. Irvine, How to be a Stoic – Ancient wisdom for modern living by Massimo Piglijucci, The Obstacle is the Way – Ryan Holiday, Discourses of Epictetus, The Shortness of Life by Seneca and How to think like a Roman Emperor by Donald Robertson.

That's a whole lot of reading, isn't it?

Don't fret – remember panic isn't becoming of a Stoic influencer instead, focus on the plan. All you have to do is get through this one book at a time. You can actually do this in addition to your journal, as a daily thing, by covering a chapter or two per day. You'll soon find that – the more you read the more you'll find you are amazed and prepared to take on the world.

This is why on that final note, we wanted to remind you that we are super grateful for your trust in us and hope sincerely that we have been able to provide you with content that has been worth both your time and your effort! We are grateful for your love and support and we can only hope that you feel that we have delivered on our promise – in fact. if you do feel like we've been helpful and think this book was a worthy use of your time, please do take a minute out of your busy schedule (it only takes a minute, promise!) and please leave a review! We'd love to hear back from you!

Independent author

As an independent author,
    and one-man operation
    - my marketing budget is next to zero.

As such, the only way
    I can get my books in front of valued customers
    is with reviews.

Unfortunately, I'm competing against authors
    and giant publishing companies
    with multi-million-dollar marketing teams.

These behemoths can afford
    to give away hundreds of free books
    to boost their ranking and success.

Which as much as I'd love to –
    I simply can't afford to do.

That's why your honest review
    will not only be invaluable to me,
    but also to other readers on Amazon.

Yours sincerely,

R. Stevens

Resources

Comaford, Christine. "The Secret To Controlling Your Emotions -- Before They Control You." *Forbes*, 29 Mar. 2018, www.forbes.com/sites/christinecomaford/2017/10/15/the-secret-to-controlling-your-emotions-before-they-control-you/#4841d56437de. Accessed 10 Apr. 2019.

"Emotional Self-Control Habits to Make You a Billionaire!" *Gutshot*, 2018, www.gutshotmagazine.com/news/details/emotional-self-control-habits-to-make-you-a-billionaire. Accessed 9 Apr. 2019.

exida.com LLC. "How to Become a World-Class Expert (the 10,000 Hour Rule)." *Exida.Com*, 2016, www.exida.com/Blog/how-to-become-a-world-class-expert-the-10000-hour-rule. Accessed 9 Apr. 2019.

Fors, Kristian R. "COLUMN: Stoicism — A Countermeasure to Stress - The Utah Statesman." *The Utah Statesman*, 21 July 2018, usustatesman.com/column-stoicism-a-countermeasure-to-stress/. Accessed 8 Apr. 2019.

https://www.facebook.com/BusinessAlligators. "How Successful People Control Emotions." *Business Alligators*, 2 May 2017, www.businessalligators.com/how-successful-people-control-emotions/. Accessed 9 Apr. 2019.

Massimo. "Stoic Advice: Is Compassion Possible, or Advisable, for a Stoic?" *How to Be a Stoic*, How to Be a Stoic, 17 June

2017, howtobeastoic.wordpress.com/2017/06/10/stoic-advice-is-compassion-possible-or-advisable-for-a-stoic/. Accessed 8 Apr. 2019.

---. "What Would a Stoic Do? The Stoic's Decision Making Algorithm." *How to Be a Stoic*, How to Be a Stoic, 10 Dec. 2015, howtobeastoic.wordpress.com/2015/12/08/what-would-a-stoic-do-the-stoics-decision-making-algorithm/. Accessed 7 Apr. 2019.

Quora. "I Studied Billionaires and Talked to Neuroscientists, and I've Realized There Are 4 Key Parts of Making Great Decisions." *Business Insider*, 23 Nov. 2017, www.businessinsider.com/ultimate-framework-for-making-better-decisions-based-on-billionaires-2017-11. Accessed 9 Apr. 2019.

RicardoGuaderrama. "Emotion Control." *STOIC ANSWERS*, STOIC ANSWERS, 17 Apr. 2018, stoicanswers.com/2018/03/18/emotion-control/. Accessed 9 Apr. 2019.

Vetter, Amy. "4 Lessons From Greek Philosophy to Improve Your Business and Life." *Inc.Com*, Inc., 6 Feb. 2019, www.inc.com/amy-vetter/4-lessons-from-greek-philosophy-to-improve-your-business-life.html. Accessed 7 Apr. 2019.

Made in the USA
Monee, IL
26 February 2020